CHERNO SAMBA
STILL IN THE GAME

Forewords by

Clive Allen and Dick Bate

ISBN (Hardback): 978-1-78281-381-1
ISBN (Paperback): 978-1-78281-382-8
ISBN (ePub/ePDF): 978-1-78281-383-5

A full CIP record for this book is available from the British Library.

Written by Simon Goodyear

Edited by Barry Gregory

Front Cover Photography by Ernest Simons
www.ernestsimons.co.uk

Art Direction by Adam J. Evans-Pringle
www.evanspringle.com

Typesetting by Riverside Publishing Solutions, Salisbury
www.riversidepublishingsolutions.com

Printed and bound in the UK by Jellyfish Solutions, Swanmore
www.jellyfishsolutions.co.uk

Dedication

This book is dedicated to my beautiful loving wife Angerine, my beautiful children and to the late Dick Bate, my 'Football Father'.

"Put your trust in Allah our Lord with all
your heart and lean not on your own understanding;
in all your ways, submit to Him, and He will make
your path straight with His guidance."

Contents

Acknowledgements

The Almighty Allah has never let me down and blessed me beyond my understanding. For everything He has done and will do for my family and me, words cannot express my eternal gratitude.

I would also like to express my sincere thanks and gratitude to the following:

My Mother, Father and all of my family who have been there when I needed them and have supported everything I have done in my life – without them, I wouldn't be here today.

Festus Asante, for being my best friend, through thick and thin.

Ian Seddon, my agent, who supported and guided me through a difficult period in my life and became a great friend.

Harry Gerber, my coach, agent and friend from day one.

Dick Bate, my 'Football Father', who sadly passed away during the production of this book. Words cannot express the love and respect I will always have for him. I wish I could thank him now for the dedication, support and guidance he has shown me throughout my life. He treated me like a son and I will be eternally grateful to him for entering my life. I will miss him greatly and I will make him proud. RIP Dick and God Bless.

Simon Goodyear, my biographer, who spent countless hours working with me.

Toby Everett, who has been a great friend and has supported me ever since we first met.

Jonathan Dennis and his family for their support.

My loyal followers, who as physical and virtual fans, have supported me all these years.

And lastly, to my beautiful wife, Angerine, and to my beautiful children for all the love, support and happiness they have given me. Ever since I met Angerine at the age of 18, I knew she was 'The One' and ever since she has been my rock throughout all the good and bad times. Words cannot describe how I feel about her as a person and I know I'm very blessed to have her in my life. She's my world and I couldn't wish for a better woman to call my wife because she's beautiful, both on the outside and on the inside.

Thank you Angerine x

Foreword by Clive Allen

*Former Tottenham Hotspur and
England forward and former FA Coach*

I **first came across Cherno when I was a coach for the England youth set-up and he was in the Under-15 squad. He played for the Millwall youth team and from a very young age everyone recognised his undoubted talent. Along with the likes of Glen Johnson and David Bentley, we had high hopes for him.**

Cherno was a larger-than-life character and it was great to see him always smiling. He was always warm and friendly and had the excellent trait of being good around the dressing room. In fact, I'd go as far as saying he was a breath of fresh air.

The environment in which he found himself – amongst a group of footballers, away from home, who had been picked to represent their country, certainly didn't overawe him. Some young players don't take such pressure well but it was a credit to him that Cherno handled it comfortably. One of his greatest strengths was his personality and he was accepted into the group straight away – everyone liked working with him because he was a very warm and friendly boy to have around.

As a young footballer, Cherno had many good traits. He was a really skilful player for a start, fantastic technically and he had confidence in his own ability; however, he wasn't arrogant in any way. What was refreshing was his love of the game and how he really wanted to improve himself and his future career. He also knew what he had to improve in order to fulfil his potential. Cherno was always a pleasure to coach and I remember we had extra sessions together in the form of shooting competitions that showed me how much he wanted to improve his skills.

It's a pity his career didn't take off in the way he, and indeed I, had hoped. The fact he didn't play at the very highest level, especially when he had been the equal of the talented players in the group, was a shame. It's always a million-dollar question as to why players don't quite make it at the highest level. Cherno definitely had the desire and the ability to be a big player but I always thought he should have been more effective as a striker and scored more goals. Obviously there was so much hype surrounding him when he was young and sometimes it is difficult for a young person to live up to the billing. Maybe that weighed heavily on his mind.

The experiences Cherno has encountered in his younger life will make him stronger and I really believe that will hold him in good stead to become a good coach. There's no doubt he's got the passion for the game of football. In order to succeed every coach has to have that passion – not just the experience and knowledge.

As a coach myself, if I was to give Cherno some advice, I would say that he should be very flexible and understanding towards his players and he needs to realise there are more downs than there are ups in the game of football – you certainly have to enjoy the good times and be able to cope with the difficult times as well in order to be a successful coach.

I really wish him well for his future coaching career.

Foreword by Dick Bate

1946 - 2018

Former Elite Coaching Manager at the English Football Association and former Head Coach of the England youth teams

The first impression I had of Cherno as a 13 or 14-year-old was that he seemed like a lovely lad and a decent human being. He was polite, friendly and happy and, not only that, he soon became well liked and well respected among the England set-up. Cherno was never disruptive, he was a joy to coach and in the best sense of the phrase, he was a 'good lad.'

Cherno's only ambition at that tender age was to be a professional footballer and it was evident he really wanted to break into the Millwall first-team when he was a little older. He also had aspirations to go higher than that; although it wasn't a burning obsession to get to the top, he had the desire to do well because he was just a well-ordered and emotionally stable young man.

As soon as he had trials at Lilleshall at the age of 13 or 14, as head coach, along with my fellow coaches Clive Allen, Kenny Swain and Paul Bracewell, I identified Cherno as a potential England player. We soon knew his favoured position was playing up-front on his own, in a 4-3-3 formation with him as the central striker.

Cherno always wanted the ball, as any striker does but he was also willing to make options for his teammates. He was a handful for the defenders and difficult to handle because he had this ability to receive the ball, turn and run at the defence, which was a terrific quality to have as a striker. Unlike some strikers, he was an unselfish and industrious player who always wanted to be part of the play. Cherno was no Lionel Messi but he could surprise you simply because of his individuality and he had enough about him to cause defenders problems when he had possession of the ball.

It could be said that Cherno was not unlike Wayne Rooney in some ways; Cherno and Wayne could be called 'natural' footballers; they were both of a similar age and in the same group in the England set-up as 13-year-olds. Just like Wayne, Cherno would never let you down and both could be classed as pure football-minded lads, who loved the game intensely. They both gelled and occasionally played up-front together in important games. They were both hard workers and loved training and would never duck out of a training session. Wayne had his own ambitions inside his head and knew exactly where he wanted to – and did – get to. I can honestly say they were both terrific to work with as footballers and as young men they were great to be with.

Cherno as an individual was popular and well-liked by the group of lads we had at the time and was always great to be around – in fact I'd go as far to say he was a 'model' player who was a pleasure to coach.

The Trials and Tribulations of a Professional Footballer

People write books for different reasons – maybe they have a good story to tell or want to give away some well-guarded secrets – but for me it was like a release of feelings and frustrations that I've kept to myself for such a long time.

One thing's for sure – I have one hell of a story to tell, a story which may surprise a few people but one in which I've experienced lots of ups and downs; some of my own doing but some caused by others. There have been both positives and negatives in my life, but I guess everyone can say that. My life is what it is.

Most ex-players who write their memoirs tend to be established household names, but from my knowledge, I don't think there's another ex-footballer of my age group who has been through what I've experienced in their life and then documented it in a book such as this.

I have good motives for writing my story. First and foremost, I really wanted to let the world know about the life and times of Cherno Samba because my story is more than one written by 'just another ex-footballer'. Yes, my story is about my colourful life on and off the pitch but, moreover, it is about my intriguing journey of enormous early promise and the missed opportunities of the 'wonder-kid' who, along with one Wayne Rooney, was supposed to be the spearhead of England's assault on the 2006 World Cup.

I think people can accept youngsters doing things wrong because they don't know any different and it was like that for me – I was young and did a lot of stuff that I now regret. When I look back at some of my actions, if I knew then what I know now, I would almost certainly have done them differently or even not at all. During my time I've come across some people who have sought to stop or hinder my football career, but I had to learn to rise above them; I kept working hard, believed in myself and I never gave up.

My main objective now is to turn the various negatives into some kind of positives and hopefully encourage any young footballer reading my book to avoid falling into the same traps that have caught me out time and time again. It's inevitable that a few kids will experience some of the pitfalls of being a footballer in the spotlight, but I really believe that reading my story can help many more over-come their bad experiences and lead them to a better life in the game we all love.

The 'traps' I refer to are the fame and all the money that is dangled regularly in front of the chosen few, those young players who are supposedly destined to become the next 'wonderkid', 'the next Wayne Rooney' or even 'the next Cherno Samba'.

My advice for any young prospect wanting to be 'someone' is centred on old-fashioned values, that include working hard and trying to do your best.

The prospect of being famous and earning a fortune may seem glossy to some young people; the flash cars, the big houses and the women may all seem great, but football let me down from time-to-time and when you read the book, you'll know why.

Having now retired from playing the game I love, I can sit down and talk about my experiences and give advice to anyone who wants to listen; however, when you're a young player in the middle of it all you don't see the past or the future – all you see is the here and now. To the modern young footballer, it probably seems 'normal' to have money thrown at them from a very young age and I bet most of them spend it like crazy – I know I did. It's probably 'normal' for kids to be 'the talk of the town' and in the limelight as soon as they do something spectacular on the football pitch and I bet most will love it. Again, I know I did. I've been there and done it all and now I want kids to relate to my story and hopefully learn from my mistakes.

What a lot of young people lack these days is good people around them; people who actually care about their welfare and whether they are making the right decisions for the right reasons. Football agents are, in general, after their 10% and they have a bad name in the game; there are some good ones, but they are at a premium. In my career, I made lots of poor decisions and, looking back, maybe I had some bad advice too. Not only that, there are young players who are earning five figure salaries at the age of 17 and think they have made it, but that's a lie because they haven't done anything in the game at that age – I made the same mistake. To me, that's just not healthy.

Fortunately, I have come out the other end and my experiences have made me who I am today – a more positive and a better person all round. I now have purpose and aspirations in life. Ultimately, my aim is to be a full-time football coach or manager and teach kids to become not only better players, but also better human beings. Not many coaches have lived the life I have, so to my mind few could be better qualified to be a football (or life) coach than me.

If I can give something back to the kids of today, some of the things I didn't have, in terms of advice and protection, then that will be good enough for me. If I can prevent even just one of those lads from making the same mistakes that I did when I was a young player, then it will all have been worthwhile.

I would like to think that anyone reading my story will take heed of the advice I give and say something like, "That's what Cherno said and he's lived it and experienced it so, you know what, I'm going to do exactly what he suggests."

It's a tough world out there but, God willing, I will achieve my goal.

God bless!

Cherno Samba

Being a Footballer's Wife

By
Angerine Samba

When I first met Cherno, I didn't even know he was a foot-baller, and I knew him as Jason and not Cherno, but that's another story. It wouldn't have made any difference to me even if he did tell me he was a footballer, because I wasn't a football fan and I wouldn't have heard of him anyway.

The first time we met, I thought Cherno was really charming and a nice guy and I think those traits endeared him to me. Our relationship developed and we fell in love really quickly and it didn't take us too long to get married.

I remember one of our first dates, when we went into London's West End with his mates, and one of them said, "If you want anything, he'll get it for you." If I'm honest, at the time I wasn't sure what he did for a living and I didn't know where he'd got all his money from. I was quite independent and very strong-willed and was focused on studying and my career, so that kind of talk didn't really appeal to me. I wasn't quite sure why he asked if he could buy me expensive things. I wasn't used to it; that was for sure.

Since then we have been through some tough times but there have been lots of good times as well. It was hard seeing Cherno whenever he was without a club and losing touch with life. I think when you're at the top of your game, everyone's there for you and everyone wants to be your friend and tag along with you, but it's different when things are not going your way.

Cherno is normally a bubbly person with a very confident and big character, but there have been times when he was very low. This happened particularly when he was not playing and between clubs, waiting for things to happen. It was not a good situation for a young person to be in. Cherno's character meant he didn't want anyone else to see him in that state, so very often he'd put on a happy face in public so that others wouldn't know he was depressed, but at home he found it hard to keep up that front.

As his wife and soul mate, I supported him through all the good times and all the bad times. I was always there, reassuring him that things would get better and often had to convince him that the good times would eventually return. Life had to continue and I had to make sure he kept his focus and was as happy as he could be in the circumstances.

Looking back, our happiest times were in Spain. Even though being so young and away from everyone I knew made me get quite homesick, we still really enjoyed the different way of life in Málaga. It was hard for a young footballer's wife in a foreign country because he'd train twice a day and when he'd come in he was tired and very often didn't want to do anything. I think I spent most of my free time going shopping on my own – but there's only so much shopping you can do! I tried to keep myself busy as a housewife, cooking and cleaning and being there for him when he got home.

Unlike Cherno, I didn't learn the language enough to be able to communicate confidently in Spanish. Because I missed my family so much, I returned back to London regularly and this meant I didn't keep up with the lessons. After a while, the thought of living in Spain and learning the language became less appealing to me. Being alone so much also gave me the opportunity to reflect on my own life and think about what I wanted to do. I realised I wanted to return home and become a nurse. We had always planned to return home at some stage, but it was difficult to know how to go about it. A short time later I got pregnant, so the decision was made for us. We didn't want to bring up our children in Spain, so after two years abroad we returned home.

The other place we both enjoyed was Plymouth. It was a lovely place to live and the way of life was completely different to what we'd known in South-East London. We had our own house and our own space and for me, I had the opportunity to start college, which meant I had the best of both worlds and the opportunity to do the things I wanted to do.

I think many people look from afar at the life of a footballer's wife and assume that it's a glamorous one, where they have everything and are able to go to all the best places. The reality is it's just not the case for everyone. It can be a very lonely life in some ways and it was sad to see some of the things Cherno had to go through.

I've never been a stereotypical footballer's wife who mingles and gossips with the other wives after each game, carries a designer handbag and wants to be seen in the media. I've always been a fairly private person anyway, and if I'm honest I often found that lifestyle too materialistic, flashy and false. I felt I didn't fit into that world. I did go to some games and a few social events with Cherno, but that environment made me feel very uncomfortable. However, the aspect that I really loved was watching Cherno from the stands among the fans.

Maybe I shouldn't say this, but I was quite happy when Cherno packed up playing football and I actually thought he was ready to move on to the next phase of his career. It was also very important to me that I wouldn't be at home by myself all the time and that we could spend more time together as a couple and as a family. I've always been proud of Cherno and what he's achieved in his life, especially since he's retired from the game. He's come so far and has grown up and matured so much. You can see he has learned from his past mistakes and experiences and he's grown as a person, although he's still a big kid sometimes. Since Cherno retired he's been so chilled out and really positive and it's probably the best I've seen him for years. He's been in really high spirits and a lot of things have been happening for him recently. He now has a bright future and he can take his career in so many different directions. What makes the difference is that Cherno is a genuinely nice guy and he's confident about his future. That's good for us all.

What I love about Cherno most of all is his belief for his faith. His faith comes first to him. I've always said to my friends and family that whenever he got a new contract from a club or he was knocked back in his life, he always had his faith to turn to. That helped him to get through the good and bad times. Whenever he had a setback, he'd always phone me with the news, so I'd always prepare myself to be upbeat when he returned home. I'd make sure the house was tidy and I'd cook his favourite meal just to calm him down and to support him as his wife. I've always worried about him when he gets knockbacks as I don't like to see him sad, but what amazes me about Cherno is that the first thing he does when he gets home is to go upstairs and pray. Once he's done, he comes back downstairs and gives me a big hug and smiles as if nothing is wrong. Now that, in my book, is a strong-minded person.

Religion is very important to Cherno and he always says that God decides on everything – not man. Whatever happens is because God wants it to happen and it's best for you. How he keeps this strength after all the disappointments he's suffered in his football career. I just don't know.

Since his agent Ian Seddon came into his life a few years ago, it's been amazing for Cherno. For Ian, it's not just business, he genuinely cares about Cherno and he tries to do the very best for him. I can really see the difference in Cherno and it's just what he needed at a time when he was low. He needed someone around to support him and to be positive and Ian was that person.

Another person who has been a good influence in Cherno's life is his best mate, Festus. Fes has been there throughout all the highs and lows of Cherno's life. Fes was the person who kept Cherno focused when things went wrong – he's been amazing and a very good friend who has stuck by him no matter what. Moreover, he's always been there for the both of us. There have been numerous times when I couldn't talk to Cherno because he felt so low, but I've called Fes and he's helped me to sort things out. I thank him so much for that.

It's sad that Cherno didn't reach the top in his football career but I really believe he's got the potential to do something very special in the next chapter of his life and it's up to him now to stay focused and positive and keep moving forward.

Angerine Samba

Chapter 1

My Darkest Hour

"Is this really me? Is this what I want from my life?"

Picture the scene of a 19-year-old lad being paid big money to play football in La Liga and living in an apartment overlooking the beach in sunny Spain.

Well, back in 2005 that was me. At first, I thought it was great. The sun was shining, the food was great, I had the beach in front of me and, to cap it all off, the football was pretty amazing, too. For anyone looking in, I had a lifestyle most people would only dream of.

It couldn't have been further from the truth!

It felt like I'd wasted the previous three years of my football career and a golden opportunity at Millwall, but now I was beginning what should have been a fresh start in a different country, far away from my troubles back in South-East London. I wanted to be loved and I wanted to be somewhere that my ability would be appreciated. That 'somewhere' was sunny Spain.

For a start, I was isolated and all on my own in the apartment, even though it overlooked the Atlantic Ocean; I had no family or friends in Spain and my girlfriend Angerine was back home in London. Although she had spent the first three days with me, she needed to go home to get a visa, which meant she wasn't able to spend a long time with me at first. I was missing her so much that it was unbearable at times. To make matters worse, when I switched on the TV every channel was in Spanish and I couldn't understand a word of it.

Then there was my daily routine, which consisted of training early in the morning, 7am until 10am, coming back to my apartment to have a nap and then going shopping in the afternoon. That was my life really. Was that all I had to look forward to? To many, that lifestyle would seem idyllic, but to a teenager on his own, it was just the opposite. I began to think that I'd made the wrong move.

The first week in Spain was a bit of a novelty. The sunshine, the new surroundings and places were there to be explored, but I soon got bored of that. I was told by the club to make use of a local restaurant and eat what I wanted to for free, which was great at first but I soon got tired of eating alone. I hardly spoke to anyone and the only contact I had was by phone with my family and friends back in London – but it really wasn't the same and it wasn't long before reality set it. Of course, I'd speak to my best mate Festus almost daily and he would always ask me if I was OK. He tried to come over for most weekends to keep me company, have fun, chill out, and just to make sure I had someone familiar around me. It wasn't a big deal for Fes – he'd do anything to come and see me. As for some of my other friends, they'd only contact me if they wanted something. Some would even ask me if I would pay for their flight to come out to see me; I often did because I felt obliged to do so and because I was bored and grateful for their company.

Not surprisingly, my mobile phone bills were crazy, and I mean crazy. Every month I'd pay over a grand for my monthly bill. However, my phone became my best friend and it was the only thing that would give me any sort of joy in those first few months, so I guess in a way it was worth it. I'd call everyone

I could think of and stay on the phone, sometimes for hours, and I didn't even think about the bill.

While I was at home, all I'd think about was Angerine and my life back in England. Before I had signed for Cádiz, I had a near celebrity status, especially in the local area where I was living in South-East London. I could go into certain shops in the West End and the store would open for me out of the normal hours while I'd browse around and spend thousands of pounds, especially in Nike Town. I had been the up-and-coming star of English football but moving to Spain was a direct contrast to that lifestyle – and things couldn't have been any worse.

One of the reasons I left London was because I was going out all the time, not training hard enough and not giving a damn about tomorrow, but in Cádiz it was the opposite – I was training my arse off during the day and staying in every night. I was eating junk food back in England, but in Spain I was either eating healthy local food or not eating at all. My life was a series of contrasts.

Being lonely is one of the worst feelings anyone can have – believe me, I hated it. Not surprisingly, I had to do everything for myself, which felt strange because back home I'd got used to having most things done for me. Well, I was a professional footballer after all! If I wanted food in Cádiz, I'd have to go and buy it myself from the local store and trying to communicate in those first few weeks was hard. Back in England, I had people to take care of me but in Spain I had nobody to help me out and I found it hard at first. I didn't really know what to expect I suppose, and I wasn't prepared for any of it.

Even though it was my decision to go to Spain, I felt as though I had been shipped out to that foreign place because I had 'failed' back in England – failed in life, that is, and not necessarily as a footballer. That's what was rolling around my head all the time during those first few weeks.

I would very often sit in my living room looking out at the ocean and all sorts of things were going through my mind – all sorts! It was a depressing time and I felt really down. Why? I was a professional footballer earning lots of money and supposedly, 'living the dream' in a luxury apartment overlooking the sea.

I'll tell you now, it was no dream for me. In fact, it was more like a living hell!

Those thoughts spinning around in my head affected my whole life, day in, day out and it was even worse at night time when I couldn't see anything outside. Nobody at the club knew anything was bothering me because I became very good at hiding my feelings, which I know was the wrong thing to do. To my teammates I was still smiling on the training pitch and enjoying my football, but I became very good at pretending everything was cool. In fact, the only time I felt 'happy' was out on the football pitch. I even stayed longer after training, just so I was anywhere other than alone in my apartment. Sometimes I'd stay two or three hours after all the other guys had left and practice shooting or work on my fitness. In reality, I was hiding my true emotions, big time – and it wasn't healthy. Nobody knew what I was thinking or how I was feeling inside, but that was my own fault. Nobody knew I wasn't eating properly and had lost weight. I felt really skinny and it got so bad that I couldn't be bothered to walk the five minutes down the road to the local restaurant to have lunch or dinner, even though it was free. I became really lazy, which wasn't like me at all because I'd always been an active person. I didn't want to see anyone, let alone eat with anyone. I also felt isolated and scared, like a little lost schoolboy.

I'd sweat like hell at night even though I had the windows open and had no covers on me. I admit here and now that I very often cried myself to sleep and that wasn't like me either. I was having endless sleepless nights feeling 'trapped' by peer pressure to stick it out in a sport that, in the darker moments, seemed to be burying me alive. For an outsider, it wasn't easy to see how I felt that way.

Things were bad and I kept it all to myself, and that was a recipe for disaster.

I'd always loved training when I was at Millwall, well I say I 'loved training' – I loved it once I got onto the training pitch but I hated getting up for training. It was the same for me when I was at Cádiz. I trained hard every day but I couldn't understand the coach giving out his instructions in Spanish. Sometimes the coach, the Uruguayan, Víctor Espárrago would speak for long periods and I'd end up dozing off – I wasn't listening because I had no idea what he was saying so I simply found it easier to switch off. That was before I started to learn the language. Only one of the lads could speak a bit of English so he would try and translate for me, but it wasn't perfect – plus he'd only do it when I was awake. There were times when the players were speaking amongst themselves and I wasn't part of those conversations, so that made me feel even more isolated. After a few weeks, I started to realise I was in too deep and that playing football abroad was going to be more difficult than I'd first thought.

To make matters worse, after training I used to go into the physio room alone and pinch all sorts of painkillers – anything I could lay my hands on, to be honest. Nobody ever saw me, and nobody knew I was dosing myself up with the pills as soon as I got home. How stupid could I be to even contemplate doing something like that? It was so out of character for me because I'd always steered clear of taking tablets, even for a headache. If the club had found out what I was doing, I'd have been sacked, no question, but they didn't have a clue what I was up to and it went on for weeks. Having said that, I was close to being caught on one occasion when the physio walked into the changing room and asked us all if anyone had taken some tablets because he thought some had gone missing. Of course they had, because I'd pinched them, but

I didn't say anything when he asked me directly and just shrugged my shoulders as if to say, "I don't understand".

On one particular day, after about a month of being in Spain, I ended up doing something else that was well out of character for me and it is a day that will stay with me for the rest of my life. I decided that morning not to go training and to black out everything and everyone in my life; I didn't want to see anybody or talk to anybody – and I mean anybody. I didn't even want to talk to Angerine on the phone and I especially didn't want to go training.

I had only one thing on my mind and that was to take my own life.

For that period in my life I hated the way I felt – every day was the same old routine and I began to hate everything I was doing, including the football. On that day, I just wanted to be left alone. I don't know why, but that day seemed like the darkest day of my life. It was so dark that I went one step further than my normal routine and ended up swallowing a load of pills, washed down with some water – I don't know how many pills I took but it was enough to put me asleep.

I was at my lowest ebb – life was that bad and I wanted no more of it. In other words, my irrational mind had made me think suicide was a rational action.

Fortunately, one of my friends in the squad who spoke English used to pick me up to go to the training ground every morning. He'd usually wait for me in the car outside my apartment and I'd meet him there, but that particular morning was different. He had waited for me longer than normal and had apparently tried to call me several times without an answer – he'd even phoned the club so they could try to get hold of me. After about 10 minutes without a response, he knew something wasn't right.

So, he decided to come upstairs and knock on my door; when there was no response, he kicked the door down. When he managed to get in, he found me there lying unconscious on the floor. I truly believe that my faith kept me hanging on until he arrived to save me. He immediately phoned the emergency services, who took me to the nearest hospital.

All I remember when I woke up was that I hated myself for doing it. Sometimes you just don't know why you do certain things in life and that was one of those moments, but when you get as low as I did, I guess you'll do anything. As I lay in that hospital bed the sense of 'failure' spun round and round in my head and I knew it must have played a part in why I wanted to take my own life. I realise now that I didn't think of anyone else other than myself and that was very selfish of me. I'm not a selfish person by nature and it just wasn't like me to go and do something as stupid as that. I guess I just wanted some attention and I certainly got it that day, for sure – and I almost paid the ultimate price for it.

I'm normally a very strong person mentally but that episode made me realise that I was fortunate to be alive. Nobody, and I mean nobody, knew about me taking those tablets or how I was feeling inside for the period leading up to that day. I didn't mention anything to my girlfriend, my best mate, my agent, my family or anyone at the club. I had never felt like that in my life and I'd never been depressed about anything. I had so many feelings inside me: I felt weak; I felt selfish; I was angry with myself because I had a lot of loving friends and family looking out for me but, suddenly, I was lying in a hospital bed fighting for my life thinking, "Is this really me? Is this what I want from my life?" Depression was so out of character for me, but it certainly proved one thing; it can hit anyone at any time.

Once I'd gained consciousness, it was a case of talking to people at the club and telling them what had happened – and why. The club were brilliant and helped me a lot and they soon realised why I was pinching all those tablets and why I didn't want to go home after training. I was devastated that it had happened to me but, in a way, it woke me up inside and made me evaluate my own feelings and what I wanted from life. I knew my life had to change and how I viewed myself had to change, too.

When I was ready to be discharged from hospital, the club gave me three weeks off and told me to go home to sort myself out. No one back home knew what had happened, not even Fes. When I finally got round to telling him, he was shocked but I knew he'd help me recover and he said he'd come out to Spain to see me twice a month in future to make sure it didn't happen again. He stuck to his word and from that day on he visited me every two or three weeks, which really helped me to settle down.

It wasn't long before I realised I hadn't actually failed at all and what I had done could have happened to just about anyone, at any time. I believe that things happen for a reason and I remain truly thankful to God that I am still alive. More to the point, I have since learned from that negative experience, which is a positive in itself. To this day, I keep saying to myself, "That will never happen to me again" – and I make sure it doesn't because I have my faith to save me and I have people to talk to and who love me.

Some might say it's a weakness when someone attempts to take their own life – but that's far from the truth. I think people underestimate the stress that a person – including a footballer – can be under and it's that stress which can lead to depression in anyone. I was close to ending it. Nobody knows what makes people do it – you're in a place that nobody else is in and nobody can ever imagine. It's only YOU and your mind that can explain how you feel and that's very difficult. Some people just can't speak about it to anyone.

Talking to someone about your feelings isn't a weakness either – in fact, it's the complete opposite. Opening up to someone makes you a stronger person, for sure. On reflection, my advice to anyone suffering like I was would be to speak to someone about your troubles – speak to anyone. Let your feelings out of your head and don't bottle them up like I did. Otherwise, it might all end in tears as it almost did for me.

Chapter 2

Football Saved my Life

*"I can help to take this boy to the top of the game, Mrs Samba.
This kid is unbelievable. I cannot believe what I saw today"*

Harry Gerber
Former football coach and agent

I was born on 10th January 1985 in Banjul in The Gambia but Mum and Dad left for England shortly afterwards in search of a better life for all of us. In the meantime, my brother Baboucarr (we called him 'Lause') lived with our Grandma Yajay and I lived with my auntie Amie and uncle Hassan Gaye for about three years.

Gambia is a little known part of West Africa. It shares the same time zone and same language as the UK – but that is where the similarities end. It's the smallest country in Africa and its main economy has been dominated by fishing, farming and tourism since it gained independence from the UK in 1965. A third of the population live on an average wage, the equivalent of £1 a day, way below the international poverty line. You can see why Mum and Dad left.

I know it sounds like a cliché, but as soon as I could walk, all I wanted to do was to play football. I loved football so much I played it every day and night until my auntie or uncle had to drag me off the park. It was the only thing I knew and it kept me active and alive – there was nothing else to do in Gambia if I'm perfectly honest, so football was my saviour. In fact, we didn't even have a proper football to kick around and very often we'd just kick rolled up newspapers or stones around the park – anything we could use as a football. We also played in bare feet because we couldn't afford trainers, which was standard in West Africa back then and probably still is – all footballers who grew up in the Gambia will say the same thing.

The fact that African kids learned to play in bare feet can sometimes attract negative connotations in the UK, but that's just how it was, and it didn't do us any harm. To flip it around, kids like me learned how to become more skilful on the ball because we didn't wear boots or trainers. If you consider that Brazilian kids learn how to play football on the beach or on sand pitches, it upholds that argument. At the time, growing up as a kid in Gambia, it was simply the norm and the most natural thing for us to do, because we didn't know anything else.

There was no grass in the parks, the pitches were rough and sandy and we had no goalposts, so together with kicking makeshift footballs around in bare feet, it didn't make for pretty football or technical skills. I played against kids of my own age and kids who were older, it didn't matter to me because I lived and breathed for football. Having said that, I honestly believe those conditions helped me become a better player in later life because I had to work harder and longer in order to improve my game. I had no idea if I had any natural footballing talent but the one thing I was sure about was that I just wanted to play football. Those times as a kid playing football were raw and you just can't buy that sort of upbringing. It was just fun and I didn't think of it as anything else; however, I had some pedigree. My paternal father, Ali Samba, was a goalkeeper for the national team and my uncle, Bai Omar Samba, was (and still is) the highest goal-scorer for the Gambian national side, so there must have been something in the genes for me to be so obsessed with football.

In Gambia during the early 1990s, English footballers were unknown to us; we had no TVs to watch football on, unlike now when the Premier League is watched by everyone in the world. Back then I knew nothing about the English game. When I was growing up, roughly one in every six homes had a TV and most of those were black and white. Life was hard; there were no luxuries at all. Things have improved since, but not that much. I had no dreams about becoming a footballer back then – to be honest, I had no dreams of being anything.

It was always the plan that Lause and I would follow our parents as soon as we were old enough to travel so, after another few years, Mum bought a one-way ticket to London for my brother, while I stayed in Gambia with my uncle and auntie for a while longer. Neither of us had set foot outside of our hometown, let alone been to another country, so it must have been a real adventure for him. He later told me he was terrified at the thought of boarding an aircraft to fly the 3,700 miles to London on his own, but at the same time I guess it must have been really exciting. For me, I was sad to say goodbye to my little brother, even if it was for a short time.

My time to travel came in 1991. I was a six-year-old when Mum bought my ticket to London and we became a family once again. I had no idea what to expect when I left Gambia and no idea who or what was waiting for me when I arrived in England. I think I cried throughout the flight but the air-hostesses were very nice and looked after me all the way. The picture I remember most was of me boarding the plane in Gambia looking scared to death, wearing an over-sized jacket that came down to my knees – I must have looked a right state. However, as soon as I spotted my Mum at Gatwick Airport, I just ran as fast as I could towards her and gave her a big hug. It was the first time I'd seen her for a few years, so it was a special moment and one I'll never forget.

I can't remember what month it was when I arrived in London but it was cold and you tend to feel it more coming from a hot climate. I think it was winter and I was freezing and kept shivering all the way to Watford, where Mum and my stepfather

Alhajie were living. I wasn't used to the cold but I realised I'd have to get used to it pretty quickly.

From the first time I met Alhajie, I thought he was a great guy; he was very intelligent, well educated and had a lot about him. Sometimes you have that classical, stereotypical stepfather type thing going on and a lot of kids don't get on with their mother's new partners, but Alhajie was different. We hit it off straight away when we first met in Gambia, as he was already a friend of my Mum, and then he stayed in contact with her when she moved to England. He had moved to Sweden but when he found out that Mum and my parental father had split up, he decided to come and live in England.

I always knew that Alhajie would have a big influence on my life and provide me with a role model figure that I so craved as a youngster moving to a different country. Culturally, African kids are brought up to respect their elders and I was no different. I respected Alhajie – he was different class because he encouraged me and he filled that void in my life. Alhajie was always a very positive guy and he'd welcome anyone into the fold. He'd always be interested in what I was doing in school and always looked at things favourably – that was the one thing that struck me about him, he was always very positive about everything – even where football was concerned. While I still missed my real father, Alhajie came into my life at just the right time.

Mum didn't give me much time to settle into my new surroundings and she had me starting school a couple of weeks after I arrived. I woke up that morning feeling excited and was shunted off to my first proper school following a couple of weeks stuck in the house doing not much at all. We lived in Fearnley Street, Watford and it was within walking distance of the Vicarage Road stadium, home of Watford FC. It didn't mean a lot to me at the time because I'd never heard of Watford FC, so they could have been anyone. The area consisted of a largely Asian population, which was reflected in the school, and their main sport was cricket and hardly anyone played football, which was disappointing for me.

There was one strange thing about my first few days at Charter Junior School that I will always remember – we all had to sit down on a carpet before lessons. As I wasn't used to that routine I would stand up regardless, even though the teachers kept asking me to sit down like everyone else did. I cried at first and refused to sit on the floor but the teachers explained why we were doing it. I soon settled in and made some friends – Richard and Yani were two boys who were always very nice to me and made me feel at home from day one.

As the school didn't have a football team, the Year 4 lads decided to arrange a one-off game against another local school. I don't think my teacher realised I was any good at football but he randomly asked me if I wanted to play as they were short of players. Obviously, I jumped at the chance to play and was excited at the chance to show off my hidden talent at last. It wasn't a proper game of course – if I remember it was eight-a-side and we played in any position we wanted to. Bearing in mind it was the first time I'd played in an organised match with a proper football and on a proper football pitch, it was a very special day for me.

I will always remember the moment I received the ball for the first time in the game and I took it the whole way up the pitch, dribbled past the whole team and scored a goal – my first goal in England. All the lads who were playing and everyone who was watching the game couldn't believe what they had witnessed and looked on in total amazement. Wow!

After that moment, everyone began to take notice of Cherno Samba and they were saying, "Who's that kid and where's he from?" The game carried on and I think I scored seven more goals. I felt like I was on top of the world. Straight after the game, Richard and Yani ran up to me and hugged me in sheer amazement. All the parents and teachers came up and asked me what my name was. From that moment on, that was it for me – I'd discovered I had a real talent that I previously never really knew I had.

Even though I was really young and didn't know anything, the one thing I did know was that I wanted to become a footballer and I wanted to play for England.

That day got even better because as soon as I got home from the game, Mum received a phone call from my PE teacher, who said, "Did you know your kid could play football – and I mean REALLY play?" I think both Mum and Alhajie knew I could play a bit but maybe they didn't realise I had God-given natural talent. They said, "Yeah we know he can play – what's the problem?" To be honest, Mum thought I'd got into trouble when she took the call – I can't imagine why she thought that, though. My teacher couldn't emphasise enough his excitement at what he'd witnessed, "No, Mrs Samba, I mean your son can REALLY play football. I really think he's got something special." So, the next day, my teacher called Mum again and asked her and Alhajie to come to the school because he wanted permission to allow me to join a new team and train after school. They both asked me if I wanted to do that, I immediately said, "Yes," and they then agreed to allow me to train with the newly formed team.

I started playing regularly for the school from that day on – not just for my age group but also for two older age groups. One day, we had a cup game (a final I think) and it was played at Vicarage Road of all places. I can't remember much about the game or the result, except that I scored four goals and I was doing things with the ball that no other kid could do. I was very tall for my age and I used that to my advantage. Straight afterwards, scouts from Watford phoned the school and asked to speak to my Mum because they wanted to sign me up – I was eight years old and had barely played a handful of 'proper' games but I'd been scouted by a professional club already. I was on cloud nine and I couldn't believe it.

However, my dream turned sour very quickly; before I had chance to sign for Watford, we had to move away so I had to reject the offer. We moved to South-East London for financial reasons because Mum thought Alhajie could get more money working in London than in Watford. As an African kid, you had to grow up before your age and at that tender age I was pretty wise and had grown up seeing some crazy stuff going on before my eyes, experiences no one in Europe would ever see. You have to learn quickly and become streetwise at an early age, so moving away didn't pose a big problem in that sense. Having said that, when I first heard we were moving, I cried my eyes out, mainly because I'd just had the offer to sign for Watford and I had some good friends at school.

I was beginning to like England too – even the weather. As an eight-year old, I had no choice about where I lived and I had to do as I was told. I honestly thought my dream of becoming a footballer was dead – there was no way I could travel from South-East London to Watford to train several times a week. In fact, Mum and Alhajie were a bit hard on me, saying they didn't want to hear anything about football again. Mum made it quite clear I was going to the new school to learn – and not to play football. Where I come from, you have to honour your mother, so that was that, and there was no rebelling against it. Well, that's what Mum and Alhajie thought, anyway.

For anyone who knows South-East London, it was full of council estates in the 1990s and we lived on the fourth floor of the Fontenelle block on the Sceaux Gardens estate in Camberwell. That's where I ended up meeting a lad called Festus Asante, who lived on the second floor of the same block. Little did I know then, but Fes would become my best mate – as he still is to this day.

However, the first time we met we didn't exactly hit it off. I was walking down the stairs from the fourth floor and Fes was walking down stairs from the second floor and we bumped into each other. At first, we had a little 'altercation' shall we say, because I tripped him up for no particular reason as he walked down the stairs. I was always on for a fight in those days and Fes looked so tall and skinny and I thought I'd pick on him in a nice way. I didn't mean to hurt him but did it as a joke more than anything and Fes fell to the floor, but fortunately didn't hurt himself. He said, "Hey, what you doing tripping me up?" We had a little friendly tussle as kids do; then that was it.

The following day, Fes saw me playing football on the green space adjacent to the flats and he joined in. It seemed strange to become friends with him after our altercation, especially given that Fes was a few years older than me, but for some reason we hit it off from then on. It could have so easily turned the other way, but luckily Fes didn't hold it against me. Sometimes, when you see a kid play football and he's got something special you tend to take notice and I think Fes saw that in me that day. I did things with the ball that other kids just couldn't dream of doing during our kick around – and I kept doing them time and time again.

I really enjoyed those days, playing for hours on that piece of grassland on the Sceaux Gardens estate – they were the best days of my life by far because I was so raw and fresh, and had no real worries in life. I was so carefree and could express myself 100% on the pitch in front of my mates. I didn't need to impress anybody and I could do what I wanted with a football at my feet. Mum wanted different things for me – particularly an education – but I had different ideas and, even though it was just for a brief moment, I'd already had a taste of 'proper' football in that final at Watford.

Peckham wasn't exactly the best area to bring up kids – in fact it wasn't a good place for anyone to be during the 1990s. There were gangs everywhere and some were very dangerous. Those gangs would fight neighbouring gangs from Brixton and Lewisham and as some of my mates became involved, I'd hang around with them too. At that time you had to be in a gang to get yourself noticed – you had to be 'someone'. I was already a popular kid because of my footballing skills and I'd been exposed to those gangs because I was playing football with most of them, so it almost seemed like a 'natural progression'. Some of the gang members were older than me, much more streetwise and much more dangerous too. I didn't want to get into any trouble but, in some ways, I was a very angry, stubborn boy and I wanted to get my own way all the time, especially when my parents were going through their problems. The environment we lived in wasn't good for me but my upbringing probably gave me a certain edge and the hunger to be 'someone' in life.

Some people would say I had two characters; I was a very wild kid on the outside but on the inside, I was a 'mummy's boy' and the best child you could ever imagine. I was very humble, very caring and I'd always look after my Mum and do the household chores. I was also a very loving kid but, once I was with my mates, I became a totally different person. I don't know why I was an angry kid; maybe it was because of where I came from, in terms of what I'd seen in life, especially in Gambia? Maybe it was because I wanted to give Mum everything she wanted in life as she'd been through so much to keep a roof over our heads? I don't know why, but I definitely had an attitude.

The only joy I had as a child was when I was playing football. It was like a release, a release from thinking about my Mum and about our life. Once I stopped playing football, I'd start worrying about her and I'd become that angry kid again and every day seemed to go the same way. Mum and Alhajie only saw one side of me – the loving side. When I stepped out of the house and went to see my mates then the angry side of me came out and my family never saw that. I don't know why I changed once I stepped outside of the house – it's a mystery to me. I guess I wanted to show my mates I wasn't weak.

It was difficult not to get embroiled in the gang culture of South-East London. On one occasion I even joined in with one of the gang fights. It wasn't a pleasant experience and when I got back home I stopped and thought about what I'd done and decided that it was wrong and it wasn't the life I wanted to get into.

I will say this now, if it wasn't for football I'd be in prison or dead by now, that's for sure – it was that bad in South-East London at that time. I needed to find some way out of the gang culture before I got sucked into it too deeply.

My new school was Oliver Goldsmith Primary in Peckham Road. It was a mixed school and, at last, I'd joined a school that was football-mad; even the girls played football at break-time. However, as you can imagine, I found it very difficult to show off my talent in a playground full of other kids playing football so I decided to go and tell the PE teacher, Neil Kite, that I wanted to join the after-school football team. Mr Kite questioned whether I could actually play football at first – I assured him I could but I'm not sure he believed me.

When the first game came around he didn't pick me and the same thing happened for the next game but he did name me as a substitute. I remember we were losing 4-0 against another local school but something happened that I would never forget. I was standing on the touchline waiting for my chance to come on when I saw Mr Kite look round for inspiration. He spotted me, shivering, even though I was wearing a coat, hat and gloves, came over to me and asked me if I wanted to go in goal. I jumped at the chance, even though I hated being in goal, because I just wanted to get on that pitch. However, I wasn't touching the ball very much at first and I was beginning to get bored – freezing cold, standing in the goal like a lost soul and becoming frustrated.

Then, after about 15 minutes, the ball came towards me and instinctively I trapped the ball and ran from my goalmouth to the other end of the pitch and scored a stunning goal. It was something a goalkeeper should never do but I just wanted my moment to impress. It was an amazing piece of play, even if I say so myself! I stunned my own team, and the opposition but at the same time I brought the game to life. I don't think my teacher was very impressed at first that I had come so far out of my goal, but he quickly took me out of goal and put someone else in and let me loose as an outfield player. By the end of the game we had beaten the other school 12-4 and I scored 6 of them.

From then on, there was no stopping me. I had literally turned that game around, single-handedly. All of a sudden, I was the talk of the school and even got announced in assembly the following day. That was it; I'd arrived on the football scene – well, at Oliver Goldsmith, anyway.

Following that game, I started to play for my own age group, and for older teams; I was playing two or three games in a week on a regular basis, but I didn't get tired at all – all I wanted to do was play football and I could have played all day long; I was full of energy and I was happy on the pitch. My home life wasn't going so well though, but more about that later.

I met my first strike partner at Oliver Goldsmith at the age of 8. His name was James Cheeseman and we hit it off from the first time we played together for the school. It actually started in the playground, playing during lunchtimes with a tennis ball. We were doing 'kick-ups' where I'd kick the ball and try and keep it off the ground for as long as possible and then volley it to him and he'd do the same and it kept going like that. We became friends pretty quickly because of our love of football and we connected straight away and took every chance we could to play together. Even on the pitch we were telepathic and knew exactly what each other would do next.

The first game we played in together was against Bacon's College, who had a lad in their side called Billy Mehmet, who later went on to be part of the West Ham youth system. There were actually several different games being played on that particular day but all the parents became aware of the two of us playing up-front and came to watch because we were putting on such a good display, show-boating and scoring goals for fun. James and I were deadly that day and to be honest neither of us could believe what we were doing. We both seemed so natural and complemented each other perfectly and, from that day on, we became the hottest strike partnership in London schools football. When James didn't play, I would fake an injury because we simply couldn't play without each other.

One thing that sticks in my memory is that every day Mum would always give me money to buy a bottle of Maggi chicken seasoning. She'd give me a pound to buy a bottle every day, so I'd have to walk or ride my bike to Camberwell and back to buy it. It was funny because I'd see Fes riding his bike to the same shop to buy some groceries for his Mum and we'd ride back together, drop the stuff off then go out and play football on the green. The next day, and every day after that, we'd both do the exact same thing all over again. I'm not sure why Mum didn't just give me enough money to buy five or six bottles at a time – maybe she thought she couldn't afford to give me £5 or £6 at a time or maybe she just wanted me out of the house. To this day, I still eat that Maggi seasoning.

With both Mum and Alhajie working by that time, our money troubles eased a little bit and our lives became a bit more stable, although it still wasn't great. There was money coming in to cover all the bills and we even had enough to do a big shop at Netto every Sunday. Life seemed good then, or at least better than it had been, and because we hadn't seen so much food for such a long time all we wanted to do was eat it all like there was no tomorrow.

As my home life improved so did my footballing skills and I began to take the game more seriously as I got older, whereas before it had been all for fun. I began to wonder if people actually got paid for playing football and I said to myself, if I start to take it seriously it could become a job in the future and if I remain focused, I could actually help my Mum out financially. That soon became the main drive for me to improve my game and I decided that I seriously wanted to become a professional footballer when I was older and nothing else mattered – well, except to get through school.

Even though times were hard, it was a period that will always stay close to my heart because it reminds me just how far I have come in my life since those days. They taught me a lot about life and how to overcome some of the issues that have happened since, and I can honestly say the person I have become today was down to living hand-to-mouth in those dark times.

For any parent, their children's education is the most important thing in life and Mum didn't really care how good I was at football, she was more worried about my schooling. Sometimes she'd shout at me for constantly playing football and not concentrating on my education, whereas Alhajie would be more lenient and would encourage Mum to give me a break now and again, which I thought was really cool. He was an ally in those circumstances and someone who would get me out of certain situations.

Fes, on the other hand, was often to be found in the local library and would always have his nose in a book (or nine). Sometimes he'd take me to the library and I'd encourage Fes to test me on certain subjects. I think I impressed him with how much I actually knew, which I suppose was surprising really, as I hated school and sometimes missed classes to play football.

Fes liked football but he didn't want to become a footballer like I did. When we played together we'd say we were Romario and Bebeto – of course, I was Romario, who was the better player and my football idol at that time. I don't know what it was about him that I liked so much, but I'd always make a point of copying every trick he did during games on TV. Maybe I was being cocky, but every time I went out on to a playing field I just wanted to play like him and I even shouted his name out load when I scored a goal.

It was Fes who suggested we go to other local estates to play football, not just on our local patch of green space, so one day we both went over to another estate and a mate of Fes' brother, a guy called Abdullah Ben Kmayal, just happened to be there. He used to be a football coach and he saw me play that afternoon and was so amazed that he asked me to come and join his team. I did just that and my name started to get mentioned everywhere in the local area around Dulwich and Peckham, as I was involved in several school teams as well as Abdullah's.

I didn't realise it at the time, but Abdullah was quite a guy and did a lot for the kids in South East London. He basically provided an outlet for them – and that outlet was football. He took it upon himself to set up a number of football teams in the area and they attracted all sorts of kids, black and white. I may be wrong but I think he had about 20 teams of different ages. His teams were well organised and you weren't even allowed to swear. You might be a gangster or a school kid but he welcomed anyone who wanted to play football. Everyone who joined his teams knew each other and protected each other too. I don't think Abdullah always realised it, but he generated a sort of team spirit and togetherness that you don't find very often.

Abdullah was not only the guy who organised the football teams, he was also a mentor to many kids in the area and he allowed anyone to go to him for advice – he was 'the man' who would sort anything. He had time for anyone and in a way he was the elder brother I never had – he meant a lot to us during those days growing up because he really looked after everyone and made sure we stayed off the streets and out of trouble.

Abdullah was a great guy, loved by everyone and he subsequently won the BBC Sports Personality Unsung Hero Award in 2004 for his work in the community.

My goal scoring record for someone so young was insane and I was beginning to make a name for myself in the area. Everyone was talking about me and I became a magnet for football coaches and scouts, but while I knew I was probably better than anyone else, I still didn't realise just how good I really was – or how good I could become. I was a precocious talent and people stood in sheer amazement at some of the things I was doing. Yes, I'll admit that I was cocky and probably verging on arrogant at times. I had the attitude that suggested the other kids shouldn't have been on the same pitch as me. That was when I was nine or ten years old and people began asking what I would be like when I grew up.

One particular game springs to mind when I look back at those times. It was an inter-schools match and I distinctly remember a guy watching me intensely, even more intensely than anyone else was – he was watching my every move. "He must be a scout," I thought. Apparently, during the game he asked my PE teacher how old I was and he didn't believe him when he said I was only ten years old. After the game, the guy approached me, took me to one side and introduced himself as Harry Gerber. He said he was the manager of Mottingham Youth Football Club and he wanted me to play for him. Wow! I was taken slightly aback but I instinctively agreed there and then; however, I told him he'd need my Mum and Alhajie's permission first.

Later that day, Harry visited my house and asked to speak to Mum. I remember his words to her, "I believe this boy can go all the way to the top, Mrs Samba. This kid is unbelievable. I cannot believe what I saw today". He assured Mum and Alhajie that he'd look after me and said he wanted to help develop my footballing talent. He also informed them that he had experience working with children as he had worked as a youth and community worker in the Brixton area, working on projects advising youngsters from the estates and streets. I think his background made my parents warm to Harry. Alhajie, being a very level-headed person, always encouraged me to go with Harry and take up his offer of playing for Mottingham. He thought Harry looked like a genuine person and believed him when he said he wanted to develop me as a player – he also said he'd put me on the 'straight and narrow'.

Harry was a mature guy and I knew he would do right by me, but for some reason I told him I'd had a rethink and I didn't want to play for him – I wanted to carry on playing for Abdullah, which was a team made up of a bunch of lads who were all mates enjoying a game once or twice a week. I didn't know Harry and I was a bit sceptical of him at first. He'd only come into my life a matter of hours earlier and he wanted to take me away and develop me into something special. Maybe I thought it was all too good to be true or perhaps I wasn't ready for all of that, but I suppose first and foremost I just wanted to be loyal to Abdullah. Harry was having none of it and carried on making a case for me to join him and he promised me that with all his experience in the community, he would be able to help me get where I wanted to on and off the football field. It all made sense to me, but still I was adamant I didn't want to play for him, so Harry left my house empty-handed. I was playing hard-to-get; however, something in the back of my mind thought it wouldn't be the last I'd see of Harry.

Not surprisingly, I later joined the Mottingham under-11 Sunday league side and Harry became my football manager. My strike partner from school James Cheeseman also joined the team. We had remained good friends, even though we'd both left Oliver Goldsmith and I was happy because our brilliant partnership was going to continue. James' parents were good for us too. They had guided us and supported us throughout our short time at school because they knew we were something special and it continued at Mottingham.

****

I left Oliver Goldsmith at the age of 11 and went to Walworth Secondary School, but that's where my troubles began. I lasted only four weeks because they kicked me out.

After just two weeks of my secondary school life, there was a serious incident with another kid; I was sent to the head-master and the school called Mum. They told her there was no place for bad behaviour in school, so I was suspended and warned that if anything else happened I'd be kicked out and have to find another school. However, when I returned to school after my brief suspension, a similar incident happened – hadn't I learned from the first time? Unsurprisingly, I was expelled for persistent bad behaviour. I felt stupid and embarrassed – it was a serious issue but I had to accept my misdoings and move on to the next school.

Harry was informed of my misbehaviour and he made another visit to my house shortly after the incident at school. He told Mum that the best thing for me was to go to a school in another borough and get away from the troubles I was facing after expulsion from Walworth and away from the local gang culture. Harry had a son about the same age as me and he told me he went to an all-boys Catholic school called St Joseph's Academy in Blackheath. Although I was a Muslim, he assured me I'd get in there. My Mum and Alhajie agreed to Harry's suggestion and he started the ball rolling to get me in. I had no choice in the matter, so I was on the move again to another school, but from that day on I started to have faith and trust in Harry and I knew I'd made the correct decision to play for Mottingham. He'd proved that he only wanted the best for me by trying to get me into a better school. However, I wanted to remain loyal to Abdullah's team, so I decided I'd still play for them as well – I just didn't want to upset anyone.

After one particular game for Mottingham, I went home and quickly ran into the house, dropped my kit off and ran straight out to play for Abdullah's team in Brunswick Park. After a while, I turned around and noticed Harry was watching me play with my mates from the sidelines. It felt like he was stalking me because I'd just finished playing a game for his team and he must have followed me home. I didn't like it so I stopped playing, went over to him and said a few words to him. I went ballistic, "Why are you following me, Harry?" I then told him straight, "I don't want to play for you anymore. I want to play for Abdullah". I then ran off and carried on playing with my mates. I'd made another heat of the moment U-turn.

After that evening, I told my Mum and Alhajie what had happened and they then told me, in no uncertain terms, what they were going to do next. In their own wisdom, they contacted Abdullah and told him I was going to play for Harry and that I wouldn't be playing in his team anymore. I don't really know what was said but Abdullah came to me one day and said it wasn't a problem and I'd always be his friend, no matter what, which was a really nice thing to do. He also conceded that Harry was the person who could take me to the next level.

So, that was that – I had been told that Harry was the best person to go with and my direction had been set. I had no say in it but, at the end of the day, all I wanted was to play football and become the best I could, so I accepted the decision.

Not everyone was happy with the decision, though. Fes, being older and wiser than me, didn't think it was the right call. He knew Abdullah and his intentions – he was a mentor to the kids of the area and Fes thought I should have stayed with his team. He didn't know Harry and what he would bring to the table, but he felt there was something that didn't sit right. In reality, it didn't matter what anyone thought because the decision had been made for me, for better or for worse, and I had to accept it. I thought Harry was a good guy and from the start he'd only wanted the best for me, even though I'd changed my mind a couple of times.

Like everyone else, Harry knew I had talent and that's why he went out of his way to get me to play for his team. Two things he said to me turned my head – "You're going to be a professional footballer," and "One day you'll play for England." He also said, "You can do it because you've got a talent I've never seen in my lifetime." He was bigging me up for sure, but he was also being honest – if he didn't believe it, he wouldn't have said it.

After finally committing to Mottingham, we won one of the first games I played in 13-1 and I scored nine goals, even though Harry had played me as a winger. After the eighth goal, Harry, who was also the referee in the game, said to me, "Stop scoring now, Cherno. Give the other lads a chance." Surprisingly, I took his advice and held back and let some of the others score. That game was probably the start of it all getting serious – I was no longer playing for fun but I was playing for my future. I was playing to impress scouts from league clubs and that was a huge step up.

Harry ran a very disciplined set-up at Mottingham – so disciplined in fact, that he insisted on us turning up to matches smartly dressed so we looked like professional footballers. It was Harry's belief that if you looked the part and were disciplined off the pitch, you would be the same on the pitch. As most of us kids were from fairly poor backgrounds, we couldn't afford tracksuits so Harry obtained twenty or so Millwall ties from the chief scout and gave us one each so we could wear it with our school uniform of black trousers and white shirt. I didn't like the idea at first because I'd wanted us to wear tracksuits and I hated my school uniform, but after seeing the other lads wearing their smart clothes and tie, I didn't want to let my mates down, so I agreed to comply.

One of the first professional clubs to contact me was Charlton, who asked me to go for a trial with them and, if I remember rightly, I stayed with them for a few weeks before returning to Mottingham. Scouts from West Ham and Millwall then started to watch me play for Mottingham on a regular basis and they both wanted me to join their clubs. As Mottingham was one of the best under-12 teams in the area, a pre-season game was arranged for us against Millwall. We won the game 8-1 and I scored five goals. Millwall were so impressed with the set-up at Mottingham that they wanted to sign five of our players (including me) and also asked Harry to become coach of their under-12 team. Harry took up their offer and the five of us agreed to follow him to Millwall. Harry decided I should go to Millwall as he thought I'd have more opportunity to break into the first team later in my career. Harry also thought it would be a good idea as he could keep an eye on our football development.

However, my strike partnership with James ended because he was being lined-up by Charlton.

So, a decision had been made for better or for worse. Millwall was my local club, even though I was a Manchester United fan growing up, and at the age of 12 I was about to embark on a possible career with them. Well, that was the dream anyway.

Chapter 3

Football Let Me Down

"He's the best talent I've seen anywhere"

Teddy Sheringham
Former England forward

I must admit my education suffered at times but all I cared about was becoming a prolific goal scorer. One year we scored 250 goals and I scored 132 of them in just 32 games for St Joseph's Academy and I won the Heinz Ketchup Trophy, which was previously held by one Michael Owen, who only scored 97 goals in the season that he won it. I not only beat his record but I destroyed it – and I was only 13 years old.

I didn't think anything of it; I just played for fun and enjoyed scoring goals back then and I was deeply in love with the game. However, looking back, it was an insane amount of goals for anyone to score at any level – it worked out at around four goals a game and we were playing on good quality training pitches. It was a credible trophy to win because we were playing against some future stars in David Bentley, John Spicer, Carlton Cole, Joel Kitamirike and Justin Hoyte, who were actually older than me. Incidentally, the record still stands today.

I was awarded a trophy for my goalscoring exploits – I think I'd scored 16 goals in three games and I was also given a football signed by Sol Campbell, who was at Spurs at the time. I was given the opportunity to meet him at a sports café in Central London. It makes me laugh thinking about that day, because when I went to meet him, Sol signed a ball and gave it to me and I cockily signed it myself and gave it him back. Sol then looked at me, smiled and said, "I like that" and duly gave me the ball back again. I think a couple of journalists turned up and put a piece in the paper and that was probably my first claim to fame. I was a bit cocky for my age, wasn't I?

Back then, I was playing in a team who were a year above my own age and I was playing against players who would go on to become household names, the likes of Glen Johnson, Darren Bent, Anton Ferdinand and Kieran Richardson to name but a few. I would go as far as to say we had the best school team in London, if not the whole country at that time. We'd have given any team in our age group a game and most of the time we would have won. Our game wasn't about kick and rush or lump it forward to the big guy – it was pass, pass, pass and score and that suited me.

By that time, I was playing for Millwall Under-13s as well as for St Joseph's. One Sunday, Billy Bonds, the great West Ham midfielder, who was the Millwall first-team coach, came down to watch our game. He'd got the first-team in for extra training, following a defeat the previous day, so after training Billy came to watch the Under-13s with his assistant, Micky Flanagan. After watching the game for about 15 minutes, they both came over to talk to Harry and told him they were impressed with our style of play and the way we moved the ball around. We reminded them of professionals. However, they also told Harry that they were impressed with me and Harry said he tried to get his players to play football in little triangles. I think Billy was so impressed with Harry's training methods and the way he got us playing that he later told Harry, "We can't lose these boys, especially the tall striker (me)".

There was one game that sticks out in my memory, when we played at Norwich and my uncle Saliou Secka from Sweden came to watch me. In the first half I was showboating big time, mainly because my uncle was there and I was trying to impress him. However, Harry laid into me at half-time and he made me cry by shouting, "Sort yourself out, you're rubbish – stop showboating just because your uncle is here to watch you. Otherwise I'll take you off". We were losing 1-0 at half-time but in the second period I was even more motivated after Harry's dressing down. Shortly after the kick-off, I took hold of the ball, beat two players and banged it into the top corner of the net to equalise. As soon as the ball hit the net I ran towards Harry and dived on the ground and all my teammates jumped on top of me. Harry always reminds me of that game, how strong I was as a person at that age to overcome a telling off and how motivated I was to do well in the game.

It wasn't long before everyone in London started talking about Millwall Under-13s. Word quickly got around that I was banging in goals left, right and centre and scouts from bigger clubs started to turn up to the games, watching me very closely. More to the point, that was probably the first time my head got turned.

There were five of us who were linked very closely with Harry in that side and we all felt that we were destined to become 'the future of Millwall FC'. There was myself, Alex Tiesse (striker), Jermaine Adan (right-back), Charles Funna (right-back/centre-back) and Goma Lambu (winger) and we were untouchable in those days – we would have made the spine of any team and we all clicked. It was like a small family in a way and we were all unbelievable footballers. The whole country was talking about our team – we were that good. Those guys were not only my best mates but they were my support network and vice-versa. I think having people who all shared the same interests helped me. We all came from the same sort of background and went to the same school so we knew each other inside out. We were a group of African kids who looked after each other like brothers. It wasn't all about football though, because we'd go out together as a group as well. If any of us stepped out of line one of us would be there to put things right. They were great days. We stuck together as footballers and friends until we all left Millwall as teenagers. Charles left football completely when he got released, but the others all stayed in the game for a while afterwards. To say they were a huge part of my life is no word of a lie – they were very good for me and I'm so grateful for the contribution and influence they had on my life. Fair play to them – I respect them and love them all.

I was still a 14 or 15-year-old schoolboy when I was asked to train with the youth team whenever possible. My coaches then changed to Kevin O'Callaghan (Cally), Alan McLeary and Nicky Milo. However, I didn't really get used to the change because I didn't like the way Cally was with us and he'd always swear at us constantly for no reason. In fact, I found it intimidating at the time, especially as we were so young. The way they wanted me to play didn't suit me either – they wanted me to play the long-ball game, whereas with my previous coaches over the years it was different because I was taught to play, pass and move. I was even allowed to do my tricks with the ball as well but now with my new coaches I felt I was being restricted somewhat, which frustrated me.

I'd always loved training but now I found myself turning up for training late, not trying as hard as I should and being rude to the coaching staff. Basically, I stopped caring and I didn't like the way I was being treated by some of the coaches; though I must say most of them treated me very well and always gave me the inspiration and encouragement to do well. Looking back, maybe it wasn't the right way to go about it, but you do things when you're young that only seem wrong later in life when you grow up and mature as a person.

The turning point in my early career came in 1999 when I was 14 years old and it was just the tonic I needed to push my football career onto another level. I was selected to represent England Under-15 schoolboys, even though I was barely 14 years old. I remember the game well, so well it was just like yesterday. It was the 15th October 1999, the game was England Under-15s versus Northern Ireland Under-15s in the Victory Shield at Bootham Crescent, home of York City and my Mum, Alhajie and Harry were there to watch me. Standing there in line while the National Anthem was being played was frightening and I was really nervous. Over and over again in my head I kept saying to myself, "This is England you're playing for." If I remember, our team consisted of players like Darren Bent, Steven Schumacher, David Bentley and Glen Johnson – we had a strong team indeed.

I started the game and thought I'd played well enough – everyone kept telling me that anyway. As I walked off the pitch, I looked up into the stands and saw Harry and he shook his head, as if he was disappointed in the way I had played. I then got changed and got onto the team bus to head back to the hotel. When we arrived at the hotel, I went straight up to my room and cried my eyes out because I thought I'd let Harry down. I then called Mum and she gave some me words of encouragement and cheered me up somewhat. However, I also phoned Harry and he gave me grief, saying I hadn't played well as he pointed out I should have scored at least once and I'd missed a couple of good chances. He also said I didn't work hard enough for the team. I was a bit confused to say the least.

My next game for England Schoolboys Under-15s was a few weeks later against Wales. Again, I was nervous beforehand and I couldn't wait until the game started. I worked my socks off in that game and during the first-half I picked up the ball in my own half, beat their defender and hit the ball into the back of the net. The small crowd went crazy and I ran to the England bench to thank the coaches. We won the game 3-1 if I recall correctly. At the end of the game, as I walked back to the changing room I looked up into the stand where Mum, Alhajie and Harry were seated and I spotted them all clapping. This time, Harry winked at me and I felt pleased with myself as I walked to the changing room to get changed. I then made my way to the players' lounge where I met them all. Harry saw me first, shook my hand and said, "Well done. That's more like it. You played well today." Mum and Alhajie then looked at me and smiled. I remained happy all the way back to the team hotel.

I also remember Sky Sports constantly repeated the clip of me scoring that goal for the rest of the Victory Shield championship that year, so my profile was enhanced even further.

After that Wales game, all the 'big boys' were looking at me – Liverpool, Arsenal and Manchester United all sent scouts to watch me and some other traditionally big clubs like Leeds were also interested. I knew there were scouts about but at the time I didn't know they were there to watch me in particular. The one time I did know a scout was watching me was when I recognised Steve Heighway from Liverpool.

The interest from those clubs was so intense that a few months later, having watched me play for England, I was invited by Liverpool, Manchester United and Leeds United, with permission from Millwall, to have a trial with them in the hope I'd sign for their team. I was informed that there were many clubs interested in me and I was asked to choose the three that I preferred. The first club to invite me was Liverpool. I remember the first thing Gérard Houllier said to me when I met with him, "Who is your favourite player at Liverpool?" I had no hesitation is answering, "Michael Owen." It didn't take long for him to get Michael to accompany me around their training ground at Melwood and introduce me to the players. Michael bigged the club up and said things like, "This is the best club to come to, we'll look after you here. Come to Liverpool, Cherno". Michael was lovely and introduced me to Robbie Fowler, who was also very nice to me. I left Liverpool that day very excited about joining one of the biggest clubs in England, but I told them I had other clubs to see before I could make a decision. Incidentally, I didn't tell them I was a Manchester United fan.

The next club I went to was Leeds, where David O'Leary was manager. I found David very approachable and they had a really good squad of players at the time, including the likes of Lee Bowyer, Alan Smith and Mark Viduka. While I was there, I played a friendly game against a foreign team. At one point I had the ball at my feet, I looked up and saw the player coming straight at me, so I nutmegged him but he just stuck out his leg, took my feet away and I collapsed in a heap on the ground. David O'Leary shouted from the touchline, something like, "Bloody hell. What are you doing?" The game was stopped and I was taken off to the dressing room for examination. The physio checked my leg and it was fine, but I couldn't continue. I think David was quoted as saying, "He could be a real star in around five years' time," which was testament to how highly he rated me, but it wasn't to be on that occasion.

Next up was Manchester United – my team. I trained at Carrington for the day, met Sir Alex and all the players and the club made me feel very welcome. The other club that I really liked was Arsenal. Whilst I was trying to obtain my release from Millwall, I was given permission to train with Arsenal. During that period, I met Liam Brady, an Arsenal legend and their Head of Youth Development. As with all the other clubs, Liam looked after me and said all the right things about the club and told Harry they were keen to sign me. I believe they offered Millwall £1 million for me at one stage.

However, having visited four clubs, my head was spinning and I still hadn't made up my mind. I believe Sir Alex Ferguson actually bid £2m for me, according to the newspapers, anyway.

After several days of travelling to visit those clubs, I went back to Millwall and was called up for England duty. Straight after a friendly game, I went back to visit Liverpool again. In one of those surreal moments, I was on the school bus one day and my mobile phone rang – it was only Michael Owen! My mates didn't believe me that I was actually talking to 'The Michael Owen' and they ribbed me big time. Some of them even phoned

Harry to ask if it was true. Guys, it happened, I'm telling you!!
Michael was calling to try to persuade me to sign for Liverpool.
He knew what I could do and he did all he could to talk me into
signing for them. After that call, I visited Liverpool again and
they really made an extra effort to persuade me to sign – it was
very special. Michael and Robbie looked after me again and
Sammy Lee, the assistant manager, asked me to take part in
a training session. During that session, I received the ball and
Christian Ziege came in to challenge me for the ball but I nicked
it past him, however Ziege left his foot in and BANG! I felt
the impact of his tackle but I got straight back up, but Gérard
Houllier went ballistic at Ziege, "Hey, what's this? Do you want
to kill him? We want to sign him! Don't ever do that again!!" At
that point I got a bit scared that he had injured me but fortunately I was able to carry on playing.

After that training game, I sat in between Robbie Fowler and
Emile Heskey and Emile took me to one side and said, in a
joking way, "I hope you come and sign for us – but I hope
you don't come and take my place." Being a cocky teenager,
my reply was in keeping with that image, "Well, if I'm gonna
sign for you guys I hope I do take your place because I've got
to look after number one haven't I?" Who knows what they
thought of me after that comment?

Another few days went by and I was still weighing up my
options. I concluded that each had good points and each club
was different. At Arsenal, I noticed all the players ate together
and they seemed like one big happy family. At Manchester
United, I already knew Kieran Richardson from the England
set-up and he tried to persuade me to sign. Roy Keane, as club
captain, did a great job of introducing me to each and every
player, including David Beckham, who was great.

During the period that I was visiting those clubs, Nike
invited me to the Arsenal training ground at London Colney
along with another ten lads, including Craig Holloway, Joel
Kitamirike, Jermaine Jenas and Jermaine Pennant. We were

all sponsored by Nike and were selected as being the best 16 to 19-year-olds in the country and we had the honour of meeting the Brazil national side, who were using the training facilities before an international friendly with Wales. I was really excited because I thought I'd be in with a chance of meeting one of my football idols, Ronaldo (the original one). The great man wasn't there but the likes of Rivaldo, Roberto Carlos and Denilson were and I got to watch them train and meet them.

It was the first time I saw a big-named player like Rivaldo actually go around the training ground to pick up every single cone that was used in the training. He was the FIFA Player of the Year and had just won the Ballon d'Or, so can you imagine what an impression that had on me as a 15-year old? It changed my perspective of the game, how I viewed superstars and perhaps how I viewed life in general. I stood there watching him do those things and I thought, "Wow, he's the world's best player and he's picking up cones. Why's he doing that?" His humility was very humbling, watching such a legend do something like that. Footballers typically have everything laid out and done for them but here was Rivaldo doing something he really didn't have to do. If you went to any training ground in the country, you'd rarely see senior players do anything like that, so it really stuck in my memory. Even if I didn't go away from there and copy him exactly, it is something I will keep in my locker for when I become a coach in the future.

Liverpool were just brilliant in the way they conducted themselves and tried to 'sell' the club to me from day one, and for me as a 15-year old schoolboy, they stood out by a mile. It was during March 2000 that Liverpool apparently bid £1.5m for me, a deal which would have made me the most expensive schoolboy in the country. I'd been to all four clubs once or twice each and I had to make my mind up. In my head, I'd decided it was Liverpool and even before I went up there for the second time to have another look, it was all over the media. They saw me wearing a Liverpool jacket during my second visit and things went crazy, with everyone assuming that I had signed for Liverpool.

A few days after returning to London, I remember there were helicopters flying over my estate and everyone at school was all over me, asking me what was happening. I think some people thought I'd chosen Arsenal for some reason, maybe because it was a London club; while they appealed to me a lot, I only wanted to sign for Liverpool. Arsene Wenger was charming and told me the same stuff as every other manager, but I think the reason why they didn't make too much of a fuss over me was that they had recently signed Jermaine Pennant from Notts County, who I think had just become the country's most expensive teenager at that time. However, I felt as though I couldn't let Michael Owen down as he'd spent a lot of time trying to get me to join, so I told Liverpool they were going to be my club.

I later informed Millwall that I had chosen to join Liverpool. Everything was moving on nicely and I had hoped the two clubs were going to finalise the deal quickly. The fee they were prepared to pay for me, a 15-year old, was huge but being so young I didn't care about the money – I just wanted to play for Liverpool FC. It was a big, Premier League club and I wanted to step up a level or two – that was the main motivation for me. I am not sure of the financial package Liverpool were offering me once I signed professional, because no personal terms were discussed, but I was told it could have been mind-boggling because of my profile. On top of the salary, there would have been other incentives like accommodation and tutoring, as my parents were very conscious of the effect my football was having on my education, so that was non-negotiable. I couldn't wait to become 17 years old, that was for sure, but I wanted to prove myself on a bigger stage most of all – the Premier League. A headline in one newspaper read:

BOY AGED 15 WITH THE PRICE TAG OF £1.5 MILLION

Another one read:

JUST 15 AND HE'S WORTH £1.5M

I was being talked about by a lot of people. Teddy Sheringham was quoted as saying, "He's the best talent I've seen anywhere."

On the subject of money, you're not supposed to get paid by a football club until the age of 16 or 17. I was constantly being approached by agents who wanted me to play for some of the top clubs in the Premier League. Everyone wanted me – I was the most wanted kid in England and I could have jumped on the bandwagon. I even had a visit one day from the leading sports agent at the time, who said he could take me to a big London club and offered Alhajie a huge amount of money (around £25,000). Alhajie told him he couldn't understand why he should be paying him to look after me, "Isn't it supposed to be the other way round? Shouldn't we pay you to look after our son?"

My parents weren't earning very much money, so that was a massive amount. However, they declined the offer as they felt it wasn't the right thing to do – they just didn't understand the concept. Alhajie was only earning £1,000 a month and the money on offer was very tempting, but in the end he thought that wouldn't be to my advantage. I think he thought if he took the money he would be betraying me. It was a big decision to make and a lot of money to turn down, especially when we needed it, but we were a family unit so the decision was made between us, plus Alhajie was a man of principles and he wouldn't allow money to influence any decision.

Eventually news broke that I would be signing for Liverpool and camera crews began to follow my every move. It got so bad that Steve Heighway advised us to go and check into a hotel until the frenzy died down. The coverage was insane, both in London and Liverpool.

What I didn't realise back then is that things aren't always plain sailing in football and, just as everyone thought it was a done-deal, Millwall made it clear they didn't want to let me go – even for £1.5m. They rated me that highly and were standing firm. I was their jewel and they weren't going to let me go lightly. I had no idea what negotiations were going on between the two clubs behind my back, but I was beginning to tell all my friends I had been transferred to Liverpool for £1.5m. Fes was telling everyone and so were my parents and we all got very excited. I even phoned my (then) girlfriend and her parents to tell them I was about to become a Liverpool player. For a couple of weeks after agreeing to sign in principle, we were back and forth to Liverpool while the disagreements behind the scenes were hopefully being resolved.

I'd been buzzing for the previous few weeks but something at the back of my mind began to tell me it wasn't going to go through. I later learned that the two clubs were in deadlock and neither side would change their stance, but at the time I had no insight to what was happening behind the scenes. I was informed that those disagreements were apparently over the way the transfer was paid and the Millwall chairman, Theo Paphitis (from Dragons' Den) allegedly wanted the whole £1.5m in one lump sum. Liverpool wouldn't budge and nor would Millwall. Both clubs were fighting for me and I was stuck in the middle. In all honesty, although Millwall was my club and I loved them, I became frustrated that I couldn't follow my dreams. I had made up my mind and had begun dreaming of playing for Liverpool by this point, but it was looking more and more likely I would remain at The Den.

You can't imagine how that felt for a 15-year-old boy who just wanted to play football.

I remember meeting Gérard Houllier while the wrangling was going on and he said to me, "Son, we want you. We want to sign you. What we are going to do is go away and we're going to think about it and come back to you. Ok? Son, we want you. Don't worry". When I heard those words, "Don't worry," I knew it wasn't going to happen, so much so that I was almost in tears after I'd spoken with Mr Houllier.

Harry saw me with my face in my hands and held me and said, "Listen Cherno, don't worry. Everything will be all right. We'll sort it out". Although he tried to comfort me and put me at ease, he wasn't telling me what was going on or what was causing this situation, but I knew something wasn't right. It was those words, "Don't worry," again, that sent alarm bells ringing in my head.

A week later, I still hadn't heard anything from the club or from Harry. Little did I know at the time, but the deal was already dead; my mother knew; Harry knew and everyone seemed to know apart from me. I'd been left in the dark. I later found out that Mum and Alhajie couldn't say anything because she knew I would be so upset if she had told me. Then one day, when I came back from school, Alhajie took me into the kitchen, explained everything and said that everyone was devastated for me. When he'd finished explaining, I dropped to the floor and cried my eyes out. Mum came downstairs and said simply, "Son, that's life I'm afraid." I was devastated and became withdrawn from everyone and everything after that and I think my football was affected too, because I started to lose confidence in my own ability.

While all the wrangling had been going on, Harry advised me to stay away from Millwall in the hope that the club would reconsider their stance. As this didn't happen, he took legal advice and promised he'd get me the opportunity to live my dream if it was at all possible. In hindsight, that was probably the wrong move because I wasn't exactly flavour of the month at Millwall and I was basically left without a club. Equally, I hadn't carried myself very well there and I felt I couldn't go back, even though I had done nothing wrong. It wasn't only me who wanted to leave Millwall by this time – the other four lads

(Charles, Goma, Jermaine and Alex) all wanted to leave too as they had become victims of the whole episode.

Millwall knew how important we were to them and Harry encouraged us all to make the club aware that we would leave if we were not treated better. We were too good to let go. Harry had decided we needed some external legal advice so he went to see a friend of his, a famous London lawyer called Mel Stein, who worked for Clintons and in the past has acted as an agent for a host of well-known footballers, including Paul Gascoigne, Chris Waddle and Alan Shearer.

Mel advised us to go to an FA tribunal to agree a fee for me. Once the FA knew this was happening, they told me to train with Arsenal to keep myself fit because I could no longer train with Millwall. They wanted to protect me as I was an England player and they couldn't have me doing nothing while the tribunal was going on. I think I trained at London Colney for about five months, during which time Liam Brady was so impressed with me that he spoke of giving me a contract. Nothing materialised, however, mainly because I was tied to Millwall while the tribunal was happening and Millwall refused to release me.

The aim of the tribunal was to get the contract paperwork released so we could leave the club; however, the tribunal came to the conclusion that we all had contracts with Millwall so we were advised to go back to the club. In short, Millwall couldn't agree on a fee for me so I wasn't allowed to leave.

Liverpool eventually dropped their interest in me and I was told that they would wait and review my situation when I turned 18, which was no good to me as my dream had been shattered.

I ended up being away from Millwall for around six months until Mum and Alhajie eventually talked me round to going back – they said I had a God-given talent and I needed to use it. I agreed and a meeting was arranged with Bob Pearson, the Millwall Chairman at the time, my parents, Harry and myself. We met in his office and he put forward some proposals for my return. The club ended up agreeing to half of my demands in return for me resuming training. In effect, it meant I was going to be paid more than some of the first-team players who played week-in, week-out, so I was cool with that. I eventually went back to training shortly after our meeting and, in return, I agreed to sign an academy contract with the club followed by a guaranteed three-year contract when I turned 17. During the period I was away from Millwall, they had drafted in a promising youngster from the academy called Moses Ashikodi. To be fair, Moses was a decent player and had a bit about him, but I believed that I was better than him.

While the on-off transfer with Liverpool was going on, I was still going to school (occasionally) and my GCSE exams were fast approaching. My education had suffered but I didn't know where my life was going to take me at the age of 15. To this day, my one regret is that I didn't go to school more often.

When I was at school, my education took a backseat to football but it's different for young players now. One positive change the FA has implemented means clubs must put more emphasis on a young footballer's education. I guess going away with my club (and later with England) became a habit, but my education should have been a habit too. It's true what they say about practising habits – good or bad – becomes the norm. In a way, my school were more interested in the fact that "Cherno Samba's playing for England..." and they saw it as a recommendation for the school, which meant I could practically do anything I wanted. For example, if I turned up late the teacher wouldn't mark me down. That wasn't good for the other kids or for the school, but at the time it was good for me because it was to my advantage and I didn't know any different. Yes, I loved the fact I was treated differently because of who I was – let's be fair, who wouldn't? Looking back, I see it was wrong and it only hindered my education. I really thought it was 'the norm' for me and I could get away with anything; most of the time, I did.

However, it wasn't just the football that distracted me from school – girls did as well, or at least one girl in particular. I had a girlfriend who lived in Catford, about half an hour away from my house. She was older than me and I think she went to college – I say 'think' because I didn't actually see her go there because I'd be at her house most days. When I was supposed to be at school, I'd actually stay at her house and do all the normal things teenagers do and then go back home on the bus, pretending to Mum that I'd had a hard day. I must have done that for about two years. To this day, my Mum and Alhajie don't know what I was doing (well they do now) and they would have been shocked if they'd found out – and I'd have been in big trouble. I thought it was normal but I now see it wasn't right and it's an example of how people can make you think that doing something bad is cool. All I was doing was capitalising on the times I went away playing football by going to see my girlfriend. I did this day in, day out and when I got home I'd do the chores for Mum as if nothing was wrong.

It's funny that my school didn't even chase my parents to ask why I was absent from school so often. Every time I was called up for England, not only did I receive a letter but so did my Mum and Alhajie – and so did my school. I guess they didn't ask my parents where I was because it would have made them upset and that might have had a knock-on effect on my behaviour.

When I did go to school, I was so tired I'd sometimes fall asleep during lessons, even while the teacher was talking. Most of the teachers were fairly lenient with me, with the exception of Mr Franklin, the PE teacher and Mrs Osekita, the science teacher, who were both very tough. All of my teachers knew about my footballing talents but these two kept saying I had to keep my education up in case I didn't make it as a footballer. They were right of course, but unsurprisingly I ignored their words.

It could be said I had it easy at school.

****

The Millwall academy was based in Bromley and it has always been a great source of pride for everyone connected to the club and it was no different during my time there. The set-up always provided a fantastic education for young players both on and off the pitch to help ensure they maximised their potential. I should mention one person who was really good to me at Millwall; Micky Beard, the club's head of recruitment who, like Nicky Milo, was like a father to me. Micky was responsible for the academy until 2002 and he played a big part in my youth development at the club. In fact, it was Micky who scouted and brought me to Millwall in the first place at the age of 12.

One memorable game sums up how much faith Micky had in me. It happened later in my Millwall career when we played against Crystal Palace for the Under-19s at Selhurst Park and won 5-1, with me scoring all five goals. The five of us (Charles, Jermaine, Goma, Alex and myself) were just unbelievable that day. When my fourth goal went in, I saw Micky drop to his knees behind the goal, clasping his hands together and saying, "Bloody hell, kid. God bless you, my son. God bless you Cherno. Oh my God, unbelievable. You've just made my life worth living".

He went on saying some more inspirational words but all I wanted to do was celebrate my goal with my mates. There were only a handful of people in the stadium and I think everyone heard him. At the time, I thought it was nice of him to say all of those things and, looking back now, I feel proud to think I could make a grown man cry and make him so happy by scoring goals in a football match. I was humbled by his reaction. I didn't realise at that moment just how important it was, and perhaps if I had, it would have spurred me on to give him more games like that one. After the game he said, "Son, I never want to come out of your life. If you make it as a footballer or even if you don't make it as a footballer, I want to be in your life 'til death do us part'. Nice words. That's Micky for you. He always knew what to say and always made me feel special.

When I left school, I soon started to train full-time with Millwall as an apprentice. Mark McGhee was the first-team manager at Millwall and he built a team who won promotion to Division One (now The Championship) in 2001. I was immediately promoted to train with the first-team, even though I was still only 16 years old. It was during my first pre-season tour (to Germany) with the first team squad that Mark put me in the starting XI. During my first game, which we lost 2-1, I set up a goal and did my usual stuff. I played well in every game on that tour but alarm bells began to ring when we got back to England, started to train for the season ahead and Mark told me to go back to train with the Under-19s.

I was heart-broken to say the least. I didn't know what I'd done wrong and at first I couldn't understand his decision, but I took what he said on the chin.

Little did I know but I was about to embark on a period of my life I would later regret. During the months that followed, I didn't enjoy going to training and felt I wasn't progressing as quickly as I'd had in the academy. I had support from the staff at Millwall, but I was now standing on my own two feet and if I had any complaints about anything, I was told I was arrogant and had a chip on my shoulder.

After an Under-19s game, when I was playing with players who were 16 and 17 years old, I remember saying to myself, "It looks like it's all gone wrong for me." Then I began to think about my past Millwall career; at 14 years old I was playing for the Under-15s, Under-16s AND Under-17s; at 16 years old I was playing for the Under-17s and Under-19s; at 17 years old I was playing for the Under-19s and the reserves. However, now I was 19 years old and still playing for the Under-19s with boys who were still at school or had just left school, which meant I hadn't progressed in two years. I just couldn't understand it. Sure, my hunger had reduced because of what happened with the move to Liverpool a few years before, but now players who weren't previously as good as me were over-taking me and progressing in the club. That was the industry I was in, I guess, and I felt that football had let me down in a way – or had I let myself down?

In that period of my life, I told Fes that I wanted to quit football for good. I remember going to see him one day and I was so down and felt that my career had been washed away. I was having nightmares. I cried at night and I didn't sleep properly. I was walking and living, but I was half-dead. I just needed help from my best friend. I didn't know anything else – football had been my life. What else could I do?

I told myself that the only thing I should now be interested in was to make money and to concentrate on looking after my family and myself. I knew it was the wrong way to look at things but I was young and I had a chip on my shoulder – I was still thinking I should have been playing in the Premier League for Liverpool!

I'd turned into a bit of a prick – 'Jack-the-lad' – and I was an angry young man.

In the back of my mind, I knew what the club were doing to me and my fears were reinforced when I'd hear people say that Mark McGhee had been advised not to play me in the first-team or in the reserves. I heard about conversations that went on, along the lines of, "make him run" and "make him sub in the reserves". Those things were said about me and I really didn't like it.

I kept asking myself over and over again why I wasn't allowed to leave the club when other clubs wanted to sign me. I'd been told I could become a 'legend' at Millwall after my dream move fell through and that the consolation of that move not happening would be that I'd stand a better chance of breaking into the first-team quicker and at a younger age.

It felt like I was being picked on and here's an example to explain. If I turned up late for training by one minute, I'd be fined two weeks wages, whereas other players seemingly got away with being half an hour late and didn't get fined. It got to a stage where even the Under-19 coach, Kevin O'Callaghan (Cally), told me I was on the bench, so for the next game I took him to task over it, "Why are you putting me sub?" His response made it perfectly clear that he thought I'd been wrong in going to tribunal and now I was being punished. He also told me the club had blocked loan moves for me from other clubs, "Brentford came in for you on loan but we blocked it and we put Ben May out on loan instead."

I will never forget his words that day – it was unbelievable and I couldn't understand why he was taking that tone with me. I looked at him, thought about arguing with him, but went straight to the changing room instead and sat there crying my eyes out. A few minutes later, one of my close mates at Millwall, Charles Funna, came into the changing room, saw me crying and tried to console me. I repeated what Cally had said to me and Charles told me not to worry about it, so I took his advice and cleaned myself up and went off home. Unfortunately, that wasn't a one-off incident.

I was at the stage of my career when my idea of someone praising me became different to when I was a 13-year-old. While I preferred being praised by my coaches I didn't need any coach to tell me how good (or bad) I was playing or how good a player I was (or wasn't). I was at an age when I knew all of those things for myself. This became more evident during an Under-19 game when I was still recovering from a hamstring injury but was asked to be a substitute. I sat myself on the bench watching the game and what I remember is Cally absolutely killing Alex Tiesse from the touchline with criticism. Alex wasn't having a good game but Cally was shouting things about him to the bench that were embarrassing. Later in the game, he turned to me and shouted, "Cherno, I'm going to take him off in a minute, I know you're coming back from injury but can you warm up? I need you son". I went to warm up as instructed for five minutes then went back to sit on the bench again. He continued to cane my mate, who was trying his hardest on the pitch and it was hard to listen to. Eventually, Cally put me on towards the end of the game, for the last 10 minutes I think, but after the game he ran up to Alex as he was walking off the pitch and said to him, "Well done, mate. Great game. You were unbelievable, Alex".

He continued giving Alex all the 'praise' he could think of and then started shaking the hands of the other players in the team. As soon as Cally was out of earshot, I stopped Alex, held his head and said to him, "Alex, listen to me. Don't believe a word he's just said to you. I've watched the game and I'm telling you as a friend you didn't play well, mate. He was constantly caning you on the touchline. Now, tell me as a friend, did you have a good game?" Alex was honest enough to say, "No" and I repeated to him, "You were absolutely crap today so if you listen to what he's just said to you, he'll mess up your brain. It will confuse you and you'll think you've had a good game when you know you haven't." Alex acknowledged what I'd said and agreed to take on board my advice.

I remember that episode so clearly and I often think to myself that I don't need anyone to tell me how well or badly I perform, whether it be in football or in general life – I can tell myself if I've done a good job or not. It changed my attitude as a footballer and as a human being. All you want as a footballer, or in life, is for people to be honest with you. Cally was completely the opposite with Alex that day and I took that on board as a life lesson in how NOT to treat people. At that age, you can be manipulated into believing almost anything, even the opposite to reality, which is why I said what I did to Alex.

Note to self: When I become a coach, be honest to your players because that's the least they expect of you.

That experience made me recap my younger life when Alhajie and Harry used to tell me I'd had a crap game and I'd turn round to them and say, "but my coach said I did well." I was making excuses because my coach told me I'd done well, even though I hadn't. I didn't want them to tell me I hadn't played well so I'd always counter them. In reality, what my coach was saying to me was messing my head up. It all started to make sense to me after hearing what Alex went through with Cally, even though he didn't realise he was actually messing with his mind at the time. It was all a big game to him!

Another time, I was playing in a reserve game at The Den against Ipswich Town and their first-team coach George Burley was there to watch me play. I scored a cracking goal in that game from outside the box; the ball came to me, I chested it down and volleyed it into the top corner. I had an amazing game and I was buzzing. After the match, Cally hammered me in front of everyone in the dressing room, "...and you Cherno, thinking you're the fucking blue-eyed boy and giving it all that crap." He absolutely caned me – effectively for scoring a wonder goal. He said I'd had a crap game, so I challenged him, "Well no, I don't think I had a shit game actually! I had a fucking great game". He knew George Burley was watching me and made a comment along those lines, "Oh, is it because someone's watching you? If he wasn't here you wouldn't have flung it about like that and done so many tricks." I didn't even know he was watching me until Cally said.

I wasn't holding anything back and I didn't care that the whole dressing room was listening, so I carried on laying into him, "I had a cracking game, Cally, and I don't need you to tell me either way, so up yours." I then took my stuff and went into the shower, got changed and walked off without speaking to anyone. I was so angry at Cally after that game and it made me think about football in a whole new light.

A few days later, Harry called me and said Ipswich wanted to take me on loan, but they later pulled out. If I had have gone to Ipswich my life may well have been different; it was the break I needed but it didn't happen for me.

There were many more occasions when Cally laid into me but one more story sticks in my mind. I was in the gym doing my workout after training and Cally approached me and said, "What are you doing?" I told him I was doing my own workout but he replied, "No you're not, you're doing a 12-minute run." I asked him why then reluctantly agreed to do it. So I put my trainers on and absolutely ran my arse off. At that stage in my career I was an unbelievably fit guy – I could have done anything physical if I had put my mind to it. However, when I finished the run he told me to do another one. I love challenges and said, "No problem." So I ran for another 12 minutes. I hate losing and have always worked my socks off to be first and running was no different. I refuse to give up or give in to anyone and all I had in the back of my mind was thinking about what Cally would say about me if I refused to do the second 12-minute run. He would have slaughtered me and I didn't want to give him the satisfaction – that's the sort of mentality I had. While I was running, I prepared in my mind what I'd say if he wanted me to do another 12-minute run. When I finished the second one, he told me I could go and get changed but I cheekily said to him, "I can do another one if you want me to?" Cally took exception to that comment and replied, "Don't be fucking cheeky. Just get your stuff and go." On that occasion, I won!

Cally was constantly on my case it seemed. My uncle Salieu came over from Sweden again to watch me play in a reserve game and he wanted to take some Nike stuff back home for presents. At the time I was sponsored by Nike, so I agreed go to Nike Town in Oxford Circus before the game. I had to be back at The Den by 12pm for a 2.30pm kick-off so we got into Central London for when the store opened. When you're sponsored by a company like Nike, they send you a bunch of vouchers so in effect you get their products for free and on that occasion I got my uncle a few thousand pounds' worth of stuff – and I got myself some gear too.

When we got on the bus to go back home, both holding about seven or eight bags each, we encountered some heavy traffic and I was beginning to think I was going to be late for the game. We finally arrived at my house at 12pm, the time I was supposed to be at The Den. I was already late! Without any fuss I dropped my bags down and left my uncle at the house and drove to The Den. I was 45 minutes late and when I got to the players entrance, the door was locked. I started banging on the door to get someone's attention. In the background, I could hear Cally talking to the players but still nobody came to open up. I stood outside for another 20 minutes and eventually he came to open the door for me but his first words were, "Go back to where you fucking came from. You ain't coming in this fucking dressing room, you prick". He stood there looking at me and just slammed the door in my face. I stood there for a few minutes and wondered what to do – should I go back home or should I burst into the dressing room and confront him? I decided to go in and confront him, so I opened the door and marched in. However, when Cally saw me he grabbed me by the neck, pinned me up against the wall and threatened me, "I told you once to go home, now fuck off! I told you, you're not playing." He eventually let go of me and I stood there in a trance, but Nicky Milo came over to try and defuse the situation and said, "Look, go and get changed. Obviously you're not going to start because you were late but you'll be on the bench".

At that time in my life, I would have normally lost my temper fairly quickly in those situations, but I remained calm, collected and polite with my response, even though I'd just been treated so badly by Cally. "Whatever you lot want me to do, I'll do it", I said.

I eventually got changed and went out onto the pitch with the other players to warm up – in fact I stayed on and did extra when the others went back in. Nicky then spoke to Cally and the other coaches – God knows what he said to them, but he'd obviously had an impact. During the game I sat on the bench and Cally didn't even acknowledge me, let alone speak to me, but there was no surprise there. Nicky had a word with Cally during the game to ask him to bring me on and I overheard the conversation; Cally told him in no uncertain terms to "Fuck off." To be fair to Cally, all that worried him when it came to football was winning (which isn't a bad thing, I suppose) and he didn't care about how we were playing. He'd do anything to win the game – anything. So, with 10 minutes to go we were losing 3-1 and Cally turned round and pointed at me and shouted, "Oi you, fucking get up. Don't bother warming up, just get changed – you're going on". I did as I was told and went straight on.

Guess what? Within 10 minutes I scored – but I think we lost the game 3-2. "Up yours, Cally," I thought.

Back in the dressing room he started to take it out on some of the other lads and was actually praising me, "...but Cherno, I'm telling you, he showed more in 10 minutes than any of you lot did in 90. That's what I want". I kept quiet while he laid into my teammates. I knew I'd done well, even though we lost the game – I didn't need him telling me that but it made a change for someone else to get a pasting rather than me.

After I'd showered and changed and I was ready to leave, Nicky stopped me and we chatted for about half an hour. I will always remember what he said to me, "Son, you've got the world at your feet – no one can take that away. You're an unbelievable player and I think you'll go far. You're a special kid. Well done. I'm proud of you". I went away with those words ringing in my ears and the hairs on the back of my neck stood up. I drove off and put on the loudest music I could find on the radio.

I was buzzing again. However, for some reason, it also felt like the end for me at Millwall.

Those were just a few episodes of my ups and downs at Millwall – and there were many more like that. I had to put up with a barrage of abuse against me from Cally, who should have had known better and who the club trusted with my development. He should have had a better understanding of how to deal with youngsters, troubled or otherwise. Fortunately, I was a very strong person back then, both mentally and physically, otherwise Cally would have driven me into the ground. He tried everything to grind me down but I didn't let him. It also taught me that people can be fickle at times – one minute you're the villain, the next you're the hero.

I remember feeling so sad that my days at Millwall, my local club, were about to end, because when I started playing for them it was a special football club to me – and still is today. They had some wonderful people working there in the academy, like Nicky, Micky, Mark Anderson and Jeff Burnidge. Those guys would have died for the club and most of the players loved them as much as I did. They always had time for us and they always tried hard to help me and the other academy players while I was there. Without those guys at the club, life would have been even harder for me. However, there were also people working there at that time who I think were undermining their hard work and had a negative effect, which I believe caused Millwall to lose lots of good players who went on to play professional football for other clubs.

There were very good players at the club who many people thought would have a good future in football but didn't make it for one reason or another. I honestly thought that with the players around the academy at that time, it was only a matter of time before Millwall became a Premier League club, with or without me.

Football is a tough, tough industry. Some people probably don't realise that and think footballers have a wonderful life with their money, flash houses and big cars, but it can be cold and ruthless at times. During one particular training session at Millwall, I had a chat with Mark McGhee and he said he'd play me in the next game, but then he chose not to play me – he'd changed his mind tactically and it carried on like that for some time. This made me doubt myself, and my own ability.

We had the basis of a really good team at Millwall, with the likes of Tim Cahill, Stephen Reid, Kevin Muscat, Danny Dichio, Paul Ifill and Neil 'Chopper' Harris and they were all great with me. Tim Cahill especially used to look after me and give me loads of advice – he's a really top guy.

Dennis Wise was one of the senior players when McGhee was the manager and they were close. Dennis and I were also close – he would talk to me and advise me all the time. His views helped me a lot as a young player, having a football legend as a close confidant. However, when McGhee was sacked shortly after the start of the 2003/2004 season and Dennis became Player/Manager, that's when I believe our relationship changed and he didn't seem to have as much time for me.

My relationship with Ray Wilkins seemed to change too. He was Assistant Manager to Dennis and on the training field he'd join in and you could see he had something special about him – he could play a bit and in his time he was a great player. You see him on TV and he's the nicest guy you'd ever want to meet; he speaks so well of people and he was just the same on the training pitch. I really liked Ray when he first came to the club in 2003 after he left Watford but as soon as Wisey took charge, I got the impression they never really wanted me to stay at the club and I received mixed messages from them about the club renewing my contract. One person would say the club were going to offer me a new contract then someone else would say the opposite. I was 19 at the time and my contract was coming to an end – I already knew what I wanted to do and that was play for Millwall's first team or leave the club.

****

The one good thing that happened to me during that tough time was to meet the lady who would become my future wife. I used to see this girl walk up and down the street where we lived in Peckham and I kept asking if I could talk to her – for two years in fact I was chasing her, but she kept turning me down. One day, I was driving my new Peugeot 206, which was quite a cool car back then, and I saw her walking down the street. I stopped to show off my new motor but again she wasn't interested in going for a drive. I didn't give up though and I asked for her phone number; being the romantic type I also made a comment about how nice her hair looked. At last, she responded and agreed to give me her number and she also took my number – progress, I thought. However, as soon as I got home I dialled the number she gave me but there was no dialling tone – it was a fake number! I was beginning to think I wouldn't hear from her again and she was playing me up.

Three weeks later, she called me out of the blue but I didn't have my phone on me. My cousin, Buba Nije had it for some reason so he answered. I must point out that for some random reason I had told her my name was 'Jason' and not Cherno – what was I thinking? So, when he answered the phone and she asked for 'Jason', Buba obviously didn't know who 'Jason' was so said she'd called the wrong number. When he told me she'd called asking for the fake name, I couldn't believe my luck and called him a "dick" or "nugget" or something along those lines. To make matters worse, her number appeared as 'private number' so I couldn't even call her back. That same day, she called my mobile again and for a second time I missed the call. I was getting annoyed and thinking it wasn't going to happen.

Call it fate or destiny, but I was meant to be with that girl because she rang me again, for the third time, at around midnight on that same night. I picked up the call and we spoke at last.

If anything, she seemed keen, which was good because I was even more so. She told me her name was Angerine and we started to chat, though for some reason I was still using the name 'Jason' – don't ask me why. Maybe if I had told Angerine my real name, there might have been a chance she'd know I was a footballer. Anyway, that night we spoke non-stop for three hours and it was as if we'd been friends for years. It was the first time we'd actually had a proper conversation – it was amazing and even then I knew she was 'the one'. Everything about the conversation was amazing. We spoke about each other's lives, although I didn't tell her who I really was and what I did for a living – I think I told her I worked at McDonalds as it was the first thing that came into my head. Yes, they were 'white lies' if you like, but I was thinking she'd see me as some 'Big Time Charlie' if I told her I was a footballer and that may have put her off.

As we lived close to each other, I asked her if we could meet up and I suggested we go up the West End to do some shopping. Happily, she agreed. For some stupid reason I asked my neighbour, Clifford Osanze, if he'd come with us – again, I've no idea why, maybe I was a bit shy or something? On that first date, she must have thought I was a right show-off because I picked her up in my flash new car, the music was blaring out and I was probably wearing shades, too. We drove to the West End, along with Clifford, and we went to Oxford Circus to buy me a jacket. She still didn't know I was a footballer (or what my real name was, for that matter) and I was flashing my credit card around like there was no tomorrow. Clifford then asked her if she wanted anything, saying, "He'll buy you anything you want," but she declined politely. She must have thought I was the manager of McDonalds, either that or stinking rich. The date seemed to go well and I took her back home.

After that date we continued speaking on the phone for several days and I suggested we took it further as I liked her a lot, so we continued to see each other. Two or three weeks after that first date, I invited her to my parents' house. Mum and Alhajie were away in Gambia so I was alone with my brother. I wanted to try and impress her so I thought I'd cook a meal, even though I couldn't cook at the time. I'd bought two whole chickens from the local supermarket and put one straight into a pan without any seasoning and placed it in the oven, not even knowing what temperature it should go on. While we were upstairs, messing about, time passed by and I forgot all about the chicken in the oven until a burnt smell wafted upstairs. I explained my attempt to impress her and went downstairs to check on the chicken. Not surprisingly, it was burnt to cinders. Dinner was a write-off! What started out as an attempt to impress her ended up being a complete disaster. She said, "I thought you could cook" to which I replied, "Well, I can cook but we were upstairs and I didn't pay enough attention..." I'm not sure if she bought that lame excuse but she accepted the explanation. Fortunately, I'd bought two chickens, so Angerine helped out by chopping the chicken up into pieces, seasoning it and popped the pan in the oven. That meal was a lot better for sure and it was the start of a beautiful relationship.

****

The football world is a small place and people were talking about me during the time I was searching for another club. I was having trials up and down the country, all arranged by Harry, but it got to a stage where I was getting no further and the feedback Harry was receiving from the clubs went something like, "Wouldn't touch him with a barge pole..." I'd had a bad experience at Millwall and I thought I'd been treated badly there at times, but I started to think my name had a stigma attached to it and my image and reputation were damaged. In football, or in life in general, if you don't improve yourself whether it's weekly, monthly or yearly, it takes its toll on you and you get left behind. I wasn't improving as a player and I wasn't living like I should have been. I wasn't eating the right things; I wasn't sleeping; I was going out clubbing and I was doing the things any professional footballer shouldn't have done. On that basis, I blame myself because I should have known better, but I was mentally exhausted by my experiences.

People were giving me all sorts of advice. My big mate at Millwall, Dave Tuttle, who I roomed with, tried to reassure me all the time, telling me what to do and what not to do. He was saying all the right things to me, that I was a great guy and that I had all the attributes needed to be a great player; however, it went in one ear and out of the other because I chose not to take his advice. Sorry, Dave.

I was having no luck at all in trying to find another club and it appeared that someone in the football world had tarnished my name to all of the clubs I had trials with. It got so bad that Alhajie contacted Theo to ask him if the club was tarnishing my name. Theo denied the accusation, but it was quite clear to me that someone or something was holding me back. Not only that, no club wanted to pay a fee for me because they knew what had happened with the Liverpool deal and they knew my contract was coming to an end, leaving me to see out my contract at Millwall and then become available on a free transfer.

I knew Harry was advising me with my own interests at heart and I also knew it wouldn't be long before I'd find a new challenge. I had faith in Harry to find me something – and quickly. About two months before the end of my contract, Harry managed to contact an agent called Aza, who knew the then Portsmouth manager, Harry Redknapp, and had asked Harry, who was my agent now, about me playing for Portsmouth. I was ready for a new challenge – anywhere – and the further away from London, the better, so Portsmouth sounded great. I was excited about the prospect of playing for Portsmouth as they were in the Premier League at the time and they invited me to play for reserves. I went down to the South Coast and trained in the morning and was due to play in the reserve game the following afternoon.

Well, I didn't know until I arrived at the ground, but the game was against.... yes, you guessed it, Millwall. Harry called and asked me what I was going to do – he thought I should play in the game, while Mum and Alhajie advised me not to play. Everyone apart from Harry advised me not to play. However, I wanted to play against Millwall so badly, just to show them what they were going to miss when I left, so I stood up for myself and told everyone I was definitely playing.

The day before the game, the Portsmouth reserve team coach, knowing I was still a Millwall player, also asked me if I still wanted to play against my own club. I told him, without hesitation, that I did. He wasn't going to stop me – nobody was. I was both excited and apprehensive at the thought of playing against my own team, so much so I didn't sleep at all well because I was so impatient to play.

When it came to match-day, I was pumped up and absolutely ready to take on Millwall, even if it was only a one-off game, to show the reserve team coach what I could do. When I arrived at the ground to get changed I met some of my Millwall team-mates, the likes of Marvin Elliot and Jason Rose, who were surprised to see I was going to play against them. Even some of the first-team players had turned up just to watch me play, not to mention Ray Wilkins. It was a big event, it seemed.

There are times when you do things you really know you shouldn't do and if I had one regret during my Millwall career, it was the day I played for Portsmouth.... as a Millwall player. Hindsight is a wonderful thing but I can now see that when you're angry and so hurt about something or someone, it's the worse emotion in the world and leads to a build-up of frustration inside you. To put it into context, if you've ever broken up with a long-term partner, the last thing you want is to see that person with someone else. Well, that describes the mood I was in at that time. I think the word is 'scorned'. In short, I shouldn't have played in that game and maybe Harry should have been firmer with me – but it's easy for me to say that now because I was so pumped up there was no chance of anybody stopping me.

For me, wanting to get one over on Millwall so much was probably the worst feeling I could have had – and certainly the wrong feeling. During the game I was trying 'too hard' and it resulted in me getting kicked all over the place by my 'teammates' – I had the worst game of my life and it broke me. It broke me because it justified to Millwall why they hadn't offered me a new contract and why they wanted me out. I'm convinced Alan McLeary had instructed his players (my mates) to kick lumps out of me; in fact, some of them later told me some of the things he'd said before the game, which justified my suspicions. Ultimately, I let the situation get to me and I didn't show my best. Nothing went right for me in the game; the ball wouldn't fall right for me, my touch was poor and when I had a one-on-one, I miskicked the ball. When the ball came to me, instead of passing it, I wanted to take on the whole team. All the things that could go wrong for a striker in a whole season went wrong for me in that one game.

Fortunately, the Portsmouth coach knew what was happening out on the pitch but instead of subbing me he left me on for 80 minutes. Everyone watching the game could see what was going on, they could see the chemistry wasn't there and the move was never going to happen. Eventually, the coach called me over and told me he was going to take me off but at that point I'd given up and agreed to come off. I went straight to the bench and I remember thinking, "I don't want this again.

I don't want this anymore". I was questioning why it was happening to me again – why were they punishing me? Again.

The final whistle blew and the first person to approach me was, of all people, Ray Wilkins, "Hello son. All right mate. Good game – not one of your best games but good luck. What's happening with you now?" I couldn't think of anything to say, other than, "I've spoken to my agent and things are happening. There's a couple of clubs interested in me". The fact of the matter was there were NO clubs interested in me at the time, but I just wanted him to think there were. I told Ray that I had played in the game to keep up my fitness and to give him the impression I wasn't defeated. However, that assumption went very pear-shaped.

Going home after that disastrous game, I had Harry in my ear and he gave me a battering – and I suppose I deserved it. I knew I'd had a bad game but the last thing I wanted to hear at that moment was Harry telling me so and badgering me about the mistakes I'd made in the match. He absolutely caned me that night. He said everything I didn't want to hear during the journey home – and in front of my Mum and Alhajie. By the time we got back home I'd calmed down a bit; I was still angry with Harry, but moreso with myself.

The next day, I had to go back to Millwall to train as I was still under contract with them. It was a bit embarrassing but it was what I had to do. Sometimes you just have to do things you don't want to do and grin and bear it. I was my own worst enemy.

Several weeks later, I received some good news from Harry, news that would eventually see the end of my time at Millwall.

Things were looking up – at last.

Chapter 4

y Viva España

"You'll be more appreciated in Spain.
They have more technical players like
you there and you'll shine"

Harry Gerber
Former football coach and agent

I've always had the philosophy that if you're good enough, you're disciplined enough and have a bit of luck on your side, you will get to the top of your profession, no matter what people say or do to you along the way. People can play a part in your life – people like agents, chairmen and managers – but at the end of the day it's really up to yourself to get to where you want to be.

My situation wasn't helped by seeing players who, if I'm being perfectly honest, I thought weren't as good as me when I was playing with them or against them, yet all of a sudden were playing week-in, week-out in the Premier League or at the top of the Championship. Not only were they playing at the top level, they were earning crazy money too. At one stage, I'd been so far ahead of these players and I was the one who should have been the star and earning big money, but the tide had completely turned by the time I was 19 or 20. It began to really hurt me – I wasn't jealous of these guys but the reality that they had made it to the 'big time', and I hadn't, hit me hard because I knew that's where I should have been.

Unfortunately, what happened to me seems all too common and it's a massive shame – so much potential talent is lost to the game and it's an unbelievable waste. It's not just happening to English players – it happens to young players the world over.

Conversely, I've seen the likes of Wayne Rooney exceed his potential (which was high anyway) and there will eventually come a time when he burns out. It happened to Michael Owen, for example. With Wayne, he started at the highest level at a very young age and has continued to play on a big stage for many years.

To put things into perspective, when I was at Millwall, there were two players who were both in the youth team: Tony Craig and Danny Vella. They were both left footers but were very different players. Danny was amazing as a youngster – Manchester United, Liverpool and Arsenal all wanted him and he was hot property. Tony, if I'm being honest, wasn't as technical or as flamboyant as Danny and if I'd had to choose which of them I thought would make it as a professional, I would have gone with Danny.

Off the pitch, they were the total opposites too; Danny would go out partying and he was constantly told by people at the club to focus on his game, but he was a radical guy and did what he wanted. He gave up and came out of the game when he was still a youth player at Millwall. What a shame – he could have been something. Now, in stark contrast, Tony, who was a quiet lad, worked hard, listened to the coaches, went from strength-to-strength as a player and at the time of writing is the current Millwall captain after he re-joined the club in 2015 following a spell at Brentford. It goes to show that nothing can be taken for granted in football unless you work hard and focus on what you want. Someone once said to me when I was developing my football skills, "It's not the person who starts the race that is the winner, but the person who gets to the finishing line." I now understand what they mean – things don't always pan out as they ought to or go to plan for all of us.

As my mates at Millwall were trying to find their feet in the game or pulling out of it, strangely a number of foreign clubs knew about my situation at Millwall and had enquired about me. Harry had been a huge influence in my life for many years and I nearly always took his advice seriously. During that period when I felt 'lost', he encouraged me to try and get over it and told me that my football would always come out in the end because everyone knew I was a good footballer. Harry tried to get me deals with some decent English clubs like Coventry City, West Bromwich Albion and Leeds United but he also thought it would be in my best interests to get me out of the country for a while, so he was looking at possible avenues in Europe. He wanted me to rebuild my career, away from all the crap I'd been through.

One of those clubs was the French club Lille, managed by Claude Puel, who would later go on to manage Southampton and Leicester City. Harry arranged a meeting with the club and they were desperate for me to sign – they seemed chuffed that I had agreed to meet them and they went out of their way to impress me. They had even arranged a trial game, which I played in despite arriving late through no fault of my own. Claude put me on after about 15 minutes into the first-half and I did well and he was really happy with my performance. After the game, we spoke with the manager and some club officials and they said they wanted to sign me; however, they wanted me to go back to England and come back after a few days to conclude the transfer.

After my trial at Lille, I returned to England feeling happy, proud of my performance and on top of the world – I felt like things had gone my way. Lille were a top French club and seemed like the right club for me at the time as they had a history of developing young players who had progressed to bigger and better clubs. Although it wasn't the path I expected to take to get to the top, I thought it would be another opportunity for me to get to where I wanted to be and where I felt I should be. However, within a few days of being back in England, the club contacted Harry to inform him they had contacted Millwall and, because of my age, they would have to pay huge development compensation – and they weren't prepared to pay it. Although my contract was coming to an end, because of my profile as an England player the fee was higher, so once again it seemed like my status appeared to have blocked my transfer. That was a real shame because Lille seemed like a lovely place to live and I found Claude a really nice guy. He also gave me some good advice and words of encouragement after watching me play in the match.

I also had enquires from a Dutch club called Roosendaal, who were in the top league back then but have since gone bankrupt. Again, Harry and I travelled over and I was due to play in a trial game. Before the game, we stayed in a hotel near to the ground and all I remember about it was Harry talking to me and advising what I should do, but I had terrible stomach cramps, probably due to nerves and the stress of trying to get my career back on track. It was an important game for me and I was sick. It wasn't the first time that had happened but the following morning I was OK and gave a great performance on the pitch. However, after the game the club told me the same story about the compensation so we couldn't reach an agreement about a transfer. The fact that compensation was being sought for me became a real problem.

It was weird that I was getting interest from a number of foreign clubs rather than English sides; it was probably due to the fact I was playing more regularly for England against top-class foreign players and being watched by foreign scouts. Luckily, my big break came shortly before my eventual release from Millwall. Harry called me one day to say another European club was interested in signing me, "Good news. A Spanish club wants to sign you. They will be absolutely over-joyed to have you there". All I knew was that it was a Second

Division Spanish club based in Andalusia and Harry thought Spain was the best place for me to play. He said, "You'll be more appreciated in Spain. They have more technical players like you there and you'll shine." It was just what I wanted to hear, although I wasn't convinced at first. "Me? Spain? But I can't speak Spanish," I said. However, the more Harry talked about it, the better it sounded. As my agent, Harry seemed to always say the right things at the right time and I needed to be rejuvenated, both in my personal life and my football career, so it wasn't a hard decision really. Besides, I had no alternative.

I didn't know much about the Spanish game, but I knew they played beautiful football, so the idea seemed great to me and I thought it was exactly what I needed at that time. I told Harry to make it happen – and the sooner, the better.

It took Harry two months to get the deal done. At first, I was told I was going to Recreativo de Huelva; Harry thought I was going there as well but it was only when I got to the stadium that I found out it was Cádiz who wanted to sign me. I must admit I'd never heard of Cádiz, but it didn't matter because I could see a new beginning for me at the club.

I'd been through three difficult years at Millwall, which I felt had held me back towards the end of my time there. I'd wasted a lot of time in my career doing things for Millwall and not getting anywhere, so I told myself I would do this for me and not for anyone else. It was a new chapter and I wanted to show everyone what I was all about and start progressing again as soon as possible.

My dreams seemed to have finally come true and I began to look forward to the beginning of a fresh start; I was looking forward to a new culture, new food to sample and new friends to make.

I was very excited.

Y viva España – I was off to sunny Spain, and it wouldn't be for a holiday!

I must say the club looked after me from the start – and I'm not just talking about the salary. The first day I arrived in Spain, they put me up in a nice hotel and I went to watch a game as a guest of the club. I had a good feeling from the first moments I arrived. The atmosphere in the stadium was brilliant and the people at the club made me feel welcome. I met the manager, Víctor Espárrago after the game and everything seemed to be good. Negotiations over my contract had been going on for some time but the following day I put pen to paper on a four-year contract. My immediate thought was, "Wow! Happy days. This is unbelievable".

I didn't have any time to settle in because on the same day I signed my contract, I was called in for a training session in the morning in preparation for a practice match on that same evening. Apparently, that wasn't anything new and I later found out that Spanish clubs very often have practice matches during the week. I was very much up for it anyway so I took part in the test game that evening. The manager played three up-front, with me on the right of the three and I was given the number 7 shirt. I was OK with that but, wow, I worked hard during that game – I worked my socks off. I hadn't had any instruction before the match so I just played the game I knew. I was doing 'doggies' all through the game, running up and down the wing, helping out at the back and then bombing forward. However, during the second half, Victor took me off!

If anyone watched that game, they would have known that the number 7 was the best player on that pitch, so I couldn't understand his decision to substitute me. I thought I was doing well but he came up to me after the game and spoke to me about my display, "Ah, Samba, look, you're a striker. You're a skilful player but I want you to reserve your energy and stay up front. When the ball comes to you I want you to do your skills. That's why we brought you here. You're a technical player – defence is for defenders, striking is for the striker. That's what I want you to do". It all made perfect sense to me, and it was just what I wanted to hear – it was music to my ears. I didn't want to track back and defend then bomb forward like I was doing at Millwall. It suited me to stay up front, wait for the ball to come to me and show everyone what I could do.

Later on in my career, I discovered that playing the Spanish way had dented my progress because in England you have to work hard and do more than your role expects of you, whereas in Spain you tend to do what your role expects and no more, which in my case was being a striker and not helping out the defence.

Anyway, following that practice match I was no longer expected to help out the defenders and I was to stand up front waiting for the ball to come to me. It was a total change to my game but I understood the logic. If I spent time at the back, helping out the defenders, I'd have no energy left to do my own job, which was to score goals. I understand that there are different approaches to football and players are taught different ways to play the game, but I was happy with that approach. Ultimately, I just wanted to play football, score goals and do anything to help out my team.

I found the training methods over there to be really different and would go as far as to say they were more progressive. We'd start training early in the morning at 7am, and they were always short and sharp sessions and mostly consisted of ball work. There was none of the long, hard physical running that I'd been used to. Things have changed now in English football but back then the methods were so different. However, there was one strange thing that sticks out in my memory and that involved chocolate spread. Yes, that's right, chocolate spread. The first thing we did when we arrived at the training ground every day was to eat some bread plastered with this yummy chocolate spread. At first, I thought it was ridiculous but once I'd tasted I couldn't get enough of it. Being a greedy bugger, I went back for more because I absolutely loved it. If we trained in the afternoon, there would be a selection of fruits available for us to munch on before we started training. Again, at first I thought that was strange, but it was the norm so I got used to it and I quickly saw why they did it.

After our snack we went out onto the training pitch and the first thing we did was something the Spanish called 'rundo', where we'd all form a circle with two players in the middle and the idea was to keep the ball. It was non-stop for an hour. I didn't realise what a good exercise it was when I was doing it, but since I've left the game, I now realise why we did it. It was all about close control of the ball, good touch and aware-ness. I'd never done that before in England (although some clubs probably do something similar now), and it was classed as a 'warm-up'. After that, you'd buddy up with one of the fitness coaches to do some stretches, jogging and running. Stretching is an important part of the Spanish training routine – they take their time and make sure it's done properly. It's not until then that the manager takes part and discusses what he wants to implement into our game. He may talk about the shape of the team, who the strikers will work with and demon-strate a number of drills he'd like us to do. Most of the session was with the ball and all the drills were short and sharp. In England, there was a lot of emphasis on running and stamina work but in Spain the emphasis was more on ball work and skills. Most days I'd stay and work on my own or with another player or a coach, but most of the other players would go home and relax.

The Spanish have a mentality that you should play at least twice a week and also two days before a game we would prac-tice on a full sized pitch. So, every Tuesday or Wednesday, if we weren't playing in a league or cup game, we would have a practice match, maybe against the reserve team or another club side. The idea was to be active and it was meant to get the best out of the players. That rarely happened in England at that time and the result was that some players weren't 'match-fit' on match day. It's a cultural thing that happens at every club in Spain, unless you're playing in the Champions League. I familiarised myself with that routine and got used to it fairly quickly. It all made sense to me because you're always in top shape and you didn't train that much because you were consistently match-fit.

Our fitness coach at Cádiz was a guy called Lorenzo Buenaventura, who has been one of Pep Guardiola's backroom staff for many years. He worked with us at Cádiz before going to Barcelona to work for Frank Rijkaard and then with Pep. Lorenzo was and still is a top, top fitness coach – I loved that man and he was very good to me. One time, I had a groin problem and I remember he asked me, "When you go home do you stay on the sofa with your legs up for long periods of time?" Of course, I told him I did, even though I thought it was a rather strange question. He gave me some advice that no other coach has ever given me, "No, don't do that. Don't put your legs up and don't sit on the sofa for too long." Everyone else I'd spoken to told me to relax, but Lorenzo was telling me to be active and not to stay on the sofa for more than two or three hours. What he told me was simple and he guaranteed me if I did it, my groin problem would improve. Once I took his advice my groin problem disappeared. Unbelievable!

Lorenzo would always stop me from doing extra training and would say things like, "All that running isn't going to do you any good. What will do you good is sharp and intense training." He then gave me a scenario that changed my philosophy on football: "In 90 minutes, how often do you run? In 90 minutes the furthest you will run for will be 50 meters at a time – short, sharp sprints. What you need is stamina – you don't need to run up and down the football pitch for 90 minutes". I thought what he was telling me was simple but again it made sense. No wonder our players are tired out midway through a season – they run too much. They track back and then run back up the field for the entire 90 minutes.

Even in pre-season, most of the work we did was with the ball and most of that was possession work. The way they coached us on how to keep possession was playing three versus three on half of a full-sized pitch. On that size of pitch, you have to stick with your man so wherever your man goes, you go with him. You're non-stop because there were only six of you on the pitch. You don't have time to stop and breathe. That's why players don't need to run miles and miles to get their fitness. More and more teams in England follow that approach now because it's proven to work. Gone are the days when coaches would get their players to run up and down hills all day long. The only running we'd do would be in the morning, where we'd run half the length of the pitch and then jog back and maybe you'd do that once or twice. It would be that or doggies, running short sprints to cones laid out at 10-metre intervals.

Thank God for the modern way of coaching. We in England are starting to wake up to the way they do it in Europe. It's all changed now and that's got to be good for our game.

The club eventually found me a more permanent base by providing me with a seafront apartment and also found me a tutor to teach me the language, which was really important if I was going to fit in. It actually took me eight months to learn and I became fluent enough to converse with the locals.

****

In life, nothing is ever perfect and there were a few hurdles I had to jump over in the first few months. I'd only met Angerine about six or seven months before I got the deal with Cádiz, so the timing wasn't great. Furthermore, I'd only just confessed to her that I was actually a professional footballer and didn't work at McDonalds and my name was Cherno and not Jason, so she was still getting used to that. To be fair, she took it all well, had a laugh about it and we never mentioned it again.

We'd had a slow start to our relationship; with her turning down my approaches for months before we went out on a date and then it got 'serious'. I guess she was also still trying to comprehend the fact I was a professional footballer, so the decision to move to Spain must have come as a double shock to her. The way the club was at the time, and indeed the culture in Spain, they wanted young lads who were settled down in relationships so they could focus on their football, rather than spending their time in night clubs, which could lead to chaos. The coach asked me if I had a girlfriend and I told him about Angerine, so he asked me to bring her over. They were happy that I was in a relationship but they were immediately pushing for me to get married – we hadn't even lived together by that point but I thought it was a great idea and I wanted it to happen.

Having said that, my religion prevented me from living permanently with a girl before marriage so that was an issue at first. Maybe I was getting ahead of myself but I told the club that I loved Angerine and I wanted to spend my life with her. There was another problem though – Angerine had a Jamaican passport so she needed a visa before she could come over to see me for any length of time, let alone come and live in Spain. As I say, life is full of all sorts of hurdles and we faced just a few in those first few weeks and months.

I initially flew out to join my new club without Angerine and I didn't know what our future would hold – it was make-or-break I guess, but I was determined to succeed at the club, no matter what. I was flying in and out of London for the first few weeks just to see Angerine; however, after a few more weeks, Angerine applied for a visa and came out to stay with me for a couple of weeks initially.

I was so in love with her that I didn't want to be without her. We were both young – she was 18 and I was 19 and very much in love. Those few weeks were among some of the best of my life – it was a fantastic time and we both fell in love with Spain. It's true that all good things come to an end and don't last forever. Angerine couldn't stay for more than a fortnight so she had to go back to London to see her family.

As I settled into everyday life, I seemingly began to go on a downward spiral and became depressed for several weeks and that led to my near-fatal episode. My life was simply about getting up, training, coming home and sleeping – then doing it all again the next day. I had no friends or relatives to talk to about the negative thoughts I had in my head and my mobile phone became my best friend; that became very evident when I saw the bill at the end of the month.

The realisation of how close I was to death during those first few months hit home to me very hard. However, the episode I've explained in the opening chapter also taught me a vital lesson and fortunately, everything changed for me after my recovery. In the weeks that followed my overdose, I became more responsible, more tolerant, more patient and I started to accept that not everything in life would always go my way, whereas previously I didn't understand that. Up to the point when my life almost came to an abrupt end, I'd always got what I wanted – people always gave me things and did things for me but when I moved to Spain I had to do things for myself and I found it really hard at first. I even had to book my own flights home, whereas back at Millwall or England, the club would have done that for me because they did everything for me.

While Cádiz had always looked after me well, my early problems made them become even more supportive of me, more understanding of my issues and they were really concerned about my wellbeing. There was one person at Cádiz, a director called Alberto Benito Castañeda (I called him simply, Benito), who spoke some English and was brilliant to me. He was a retired footballer himself so he knew all about the game and understood footballers. Very often, he would pick me up and take me to his house, where his wife would cook dinner, or we'd go to a restaurant and then he'd drive me home. How many people would go to so much trouble to make a player feel at home? The answer is not many, but Benito did – he would have done anything to help me. It wasn't as if he lived close to me either; he lived about 45 minutes away and he did it every other day. He was so, so good to me and I will never forget that.

The one person who probably knew me better than anyone else in the football world was Dick Bate, my England coach. Out of the blue, in February 2005, Dick called to say he had some good news for me. He said, "Look, you've got an England call-up for the Under-20's against Russia. The list has just come out and you're included. That's good news. John Peacock (the England Under-20 manager) likes you and he's included you in the squad. I was so chuffed and surprised at the same time; chuffed because it was my first Under-20 call-up but surprised because I was hardly featuring for my club side. England was my saviour again, it seemed.

Shortly after that conversation with Dick I also received a call from Benito, "Samba, you've been picked for England Under-20s". The letter from the FA had been sent to Cádiz but I told Benito that I already knew so it didn't come as a surprise; it was nice of Benito to call me, though. He couldn't wait to tell me the news and he said how big it would be for the club as they rarely had any players called up to national sides, so having one of their players being called up to an England squad was just about the biggest thing that had happened to the club. After that conversation with Benito I was inundated with calls from local and national media outlets – it was unreal. As it turned out, I was the first young English player playing in Spain to be called up into the national squad, so of course it was going to attract the headlines and it was just the pick-me-up I needed.

The game against Russia came and went in a flash. I played well for 77 minutes before being substituted. Although I missed a couple of chances, I played football – something I hadn't done for a long time. It felt great just playing again and being loved. I just wanted to get that buzz back from playing the game I loved.

I'd been back in England for eight days, training with the lads and speaking English to my friends and family but soon after the game had ended I was back at the airport. I was devastated to be going back to Spain because I'd loved every minute of being back home and actually playing a full game. Even in the taxi going to the airport I didn't speak to the driver for the whole journey. I was sad and all I was thinking about was going back to the lonely house. I was so close to telling the driver to turn back to London so I would miss the plane and not go back to Spain, to do a runner and to jack it all in. I didn't want to go back, but I had to.

I did go back but I was sick when I arrived back. Whether it was the change in climate or something else, I just knew I wanted to be somewhere other than Cádiz.

****

I was born into a Muslim family and around 90% of people in Gambia are Muslim. People who don't know me very well may not realise that my faith has always been a big part of my life. I pray five times a day – that's very important to me – and I have never drunk alcohol or smoked cigarettes and I'm thankful to God for that. Those things show I have a strong mental strength, especially with some of the things that have knocked me back in life. When I have setbacks it's through my faith that I overcome them. For example, if I had a bad game, the first thing I used to do was pray and I'd forget about my poor performance. I have always been the sort of person who gets back up after a disappointment because life is too short to mope around and moan about things. I'm a firm believer that if something is meant to be, it will be.

What I pray for is what's best for me – not what I want. In other words, you can want something but it may not be the best for you. Praying tends to have a positive effect on my state of mind and makes me feel better inside. For me, it's normal but I didn't realise I was doing that until Angerine started to take notice of it. She told me in later life that it's one of the things she liked most about me – maybe because she wasn't brought up in the same sort of environment. What she said made me feel so happy and gave me comfort.

I realise that nobody is perfect but, as I've got older, I think I've gained a greater appreciation of God and I now make sure I make the most of all the blessings that come my way.

My faith is something that I don't compromise on. I made it known that my faith was important to me and I was fortunate that every club I played for supported me on that front and I was so thankful for that. Every club respected the fact that I didn't eat pork and made the chefs aware every time we ate together.

However, one player I came across at Plymouth made it clear he didn't share my love of God. There was one strange encounter with Lillian Nalis, a French midfielder, who one day came up to me and said something about my faith which was meant in a joking way but seemed a strange thing to say, "Cherno, your faith – you always go to the Mosque and pray which is nice. You believe in God but I'm a millionaire – I don't believe in God but I've got more money than you". In a way, I understood what he meant but I didn't share his view. It's fine by me that people like Lillian believe they are happy with their millions but I believe God has given me a certain path to follow. Having money is great, but having faith is better – for me anyway. Everyone is different, I guess, and it doesn't pay for everyone to be cut from the same cloth.

During a period when Angerine was back in London, we decided to make our relationship official and I proposed to her.

Well, I say proposed – I didn't actually propose in the romantic sense. While we had only been together for a relatively short time, we knew we were going to get married at some stage and as my religion forbids me to live with someone before marriage, we decided we wouldn't waste any time. The first people I told were Mum and Alhajie, who seemed surprised at first but happy nevertheless, and Mum promised to organise the wedding and a date was set in July 2005.

For Angerine, as a West Indian and a Christian it wasn't so straightforward because she had to convert to Islam, but she agreed to convert and that took a lot of courage and commitment. It was a huge thing for somebody to do in order to spend the rest of her life with me. It meant so much to me and showed just how strong her love for me was – and she embraced it all. While I didn't force her into doing it, the mere fact that she did convert said a lot to me about her as a person. It was a relatively painless exercise for Angerine though.

****

I picked up a knee injury during training at the latter part of my first season. I'd felt it niggling at me and if I'd been more honest with myself, I would have highlighted it to the physio earlier, because ultimately the injury put paid to me playing for Cádiz for a long while.

Certain movements off the ball resulted in some pain but I just carried on, which in hindsight wasn't the best thing I could have done. The pain was too much in the end and I decided to highlight it to the physio and that's when they advised me to go for a scan. It revealed I'd done my meniscus. I was crocked and had to have an operation. To make matters worse, I had to go to Seville for the operation, about 130km away. Until then, I hadn't had a major injury in my entire career that had taken me out of the game for more than two weeks. Looking back though, I'd had a niggling pain on that same knee for about two years when I was at Millwall but I'd overlooked it and just got on with playing. I'd had a few occasional injections and received tablets to relieve the pain, but it didn't keep me out of the game for long periods. The pain seemed to come and go but I suddenly faced a long lay-off at a critical time in my career – just when I was starting to feel good about my football again.

At the time of my operation, Angerine had to return to London again so I went into hospital alone and during the time I was there, nobody visited. Fes wasn't in the country and I began to feel down again – the feelings I had during those dark days when I first arrived in Spain returned. I was beginning to feel lonely and depressed again – I was homesick and missing my wife. I just wanted to go back home but I was stuck in a Spanish hospital, miles away from our home in Cádiz.

The only thing that kept me from taking an overdose for the second time was my faith, together with the experience of going through depression once before. I told myself, and God, I didn't want to go through that sort of thing again. I also knew I had to take responsibility for my actions and think about the people who loved me – I had learned valuable lessons from the previous mistakes I'd made.

I remember at one stage in the hospital, the nurses were concerned about me and asked if I was OK, to which I replied I was lonely. I immediately made a phone call to Harry and told him I'd just had an operation and without hesitation he said he'd be on the next flight to Seville. True to his word, he arrived six hours later and that is something I will always appreciate. I suddenly felt relieved that I had someone there I could talk to in English. On that same day, Harry came back home to Cádiz with me in the ambulance and looked after me for a while. He went out and got some shopping and made me some food and I think he even helped me take a shower – those are the little things you never forget. You never associate football agents with doing things like that but with Harry, he stood by me through all the dark days and I will be indebted to him for that. As I've said before, Harry was not only a mate and an agent, but he was also a father figure to me.

A meniscus injury takes around six weeks to heal and there's another six weeks to rest up after that before you can start training. After being released from hospital, I spent a long time doing nothing – and I mean nothing. Against the advice of the medics, I didn't do any rehab at all and went back to England to rest.

While I was recovering, the club actually did me a favour during the pre-season and told me that Málaga wanted to take me on a loan deal for the 2005/2006 season. Málaga were a big club so I didn't hesitate to agree to the move. After a year at Cádiz, the club fell into financial meltdown and they had to move me on because they couldn't afford to pay me. As part of the deal, Málaga agreed to pay my wages in full, taking the burden off my parent club, even though I was officially still a Cádiz player on paper.

However, what Málaga failed to do was give me a full medical prior to signing. I did complete a session on the treadmill with all the monitoring equipment and I passed that without any problems. At one stage, they stopped the machine and said there was something wrong with my heart because they couldn't believe my recovery after the session – it wasn't 'normal'. They probably thought I was on drugs or something. It was phenomenal and the physio had never seen anything like it – in fact, they had to check the machine was working properly. I was there for about five hours in the end and I passed the 'medical' with flying colours.

Maybe if they had done a full medical, they wouldn't have signed me.

I reported to the club on my first day and signed the papers that would make me a Málaga player. It was 11am and I was told to report for training at 1pm, so I nipped back to the hotel and had a sleep for an hour or so. Now, considering I'd had no rehab or training for the best part of three months, I was in no fit state to start proper training so, as soon as I stepped on to the training field and started to run, my legs gave way and I dropped to the ground. My knee just wasn't strong enough because my calf and thigh muscles had shrunk – they were so skinny due to a lack of exercise and eating. As soon as I dropped to the ground the physio came running to me and asked what the problem was. I had to be honest with him and with myself, so I told the truth that I hadn't had any rehab or training for months. They were obviously not happy with me and were confused because I'd passed the 'medical'.

The club knew I'd previously torn my meniscus but they were under the impression that I had done my rehab in Cádiz and I was fit and raring to go. I've no idea what my report said but ultimately I just wasn't fit – even though I was raring to go. When I saw my manager at Málaga, Juan Carlos Añón Moreno, he took one look at me and shook his head. He knew I had messed up – he didn't have to tell me because I knew it too. He said he wanted to play me but he warned it would take another two months to get me fit. To this day, I regret not taking advice from the medical team and going for rehab after the injury because I believe it hindered the rest of my career and in the end it took me longer to recover. When you lose that sort of muscle, it can be gained back but you should remember that each time you get injured your body is getting older and it takes longer and longer to recover each time. That meniscus tear I got playing for Cádiz took me, in effect, six to eight months to fully recover from because I didn't go to rehab after my operation. I couldn't blame anyone – it was my own fault but I learned yet another valuable lesson from that experience.

****

Shortly after I agreed to join Málaga, I returned to London to tie the knot with Angerine. We in fact had two weddings; a big traditional Gambian wedding on the 14th July 2005 for family and friends which was held at Angerine's family home in Camberwell, then in April 2006 we had a ceremony to say our vows at the register office in Camberwell. On the day of the traditional wedding, I was, believe it or not, very nervous and I was unsure of what to wear for the day. One of our friends Mukhlis Abdalla was working at Next at the time, so he knew about how people should dress on such occasions, reassured me and made sure I was presented in the right way – he even cut my hair. It was a hot day and some of our local friends came without realising it was a formal event, so were dressed in the normal local attire of t-shirts, shorts and trainers, while we were suited and booted – it was the weirdest thing to see. It didn't matter, though, and it was good to see them and we all had a really good time.

It's events like that when you realise who your real friends are. Another friend of mine, Kwasi Amponsa helped settle my nerves by talking to me and encouraging me in my nervous state. I have a strong pool of friends and those friendships mean a lot to me and are an important part of my life. It has to be said that Mukhlis was a tower of strength on the day, as I was nervous as hell and didn't have a clue about getting dressed up and it's those little things that make friendships special. It's one thing someone seeing that you are nervous and telling you to, "Calm down. You'll be ok", but it's really spooky when someone says: "It's your day man. It's your day. You're about to formally marry the woman you love. It's all for you."

I spoke about friendship earlier in the book; Mukhlis is a true friend and such a kind-hearted guy who is cut from the same cloth as us and didn't expect anything in return, where some of our other friends would have left a receipt for their time. Different folks, different strokes, I guess. Incidentally, Mukhlis is now a senior designer based in Saudi Arabia and is designing our house in Gambia. Knowing him, he won't take anything in return.

Angerine decided to re-join me in Málaga a few weeks after I signed on loan, shortly after our wedding. At the time, she didn't know what she wanted from life, but she had so many hopes and dreams and such a positive outlook on life. I knew she'd be ok. Angerine was definitely the person I needed in my life at that time, and still is. I had so much time on my hands I can honestly say if she wasn't there in Spain, I would have just got bored and I dread to think what would have happened to me. Angerine was the only constant in my life during that period and she was there when I needed her the most.

At first, Angerine was very homesick, but she understood why she was there, and eventually just accepted it and got on with things. It's very different actually living in a country rather than just being a tourist and I guess that was the case with us. To be honest, she didn't warm to Cádiz, maybe because it was more of a traditional town and there wasn't much to do, plus being young and black, we tended to stick out a lot more from the crowd. However, she soon fell in love with Málaga and we began to settle into the area.

At this point I'd like to mention a lovely guy called Sergio Gutierrez De La Torre, who was employed by the club to 'look after me'. He was the guy who took the burden of joining a new club off the players and helped them to settle in. His job was to find accommodation, sort out mobile contracts, bank accounts and generally do all the chores a new player would have to do. Sergio was to 'go to guy' for everything, including where to eat – and where not to eat – in the area. During the passage of time we became close and he took me in and started working for me, doing things which weren't in his job description (if he had one). In fact, jumping a little further into my career, Sergio left Cádiz and joined me in Málaga a year later as my kind of personal assistant, which included him cooking for me, cleaning, driving me around the area and he was my personal trainer too. He also found a house for us in Málaga. Sergio was very instrumental in my life and helped me immensely in making the transition into Spanish life all the more easier. When I moved to Málaga he helped me move all of my belongings to my new house. As Sergio lived in Barcelona, he'd live with me for two or three months at a time and then go home for a while to see his family. Angerine took him in as well and he'd help her with whatever she wanted. To this day we are still close and speak several times a week.

There was one player in the Málaga dressing room with whom I connected more than most and his name was Álvaro Silva. He played as a centre-back and he looked after me from the first day I arrived at the club. I don't know why we connected – he didn't even speak English – but fortunately by that time I could speak Spanish so we'd all converse in the native language. He was local to the area he'd pick me up, along with his brother, Kiki (who was a solid left-back at the club) to go to training and then take me back home every day. Very often, he'd take me to his family's house in Marbella for dinner on the beach. Both families were close and we all had some very good times together. I will always remember their mother's paella – it was amazing! I have so much love for Álvaro and Kiki that I'll always be grateful for their support throughout my time at Málaga.

We'd very often have a laugh at the club's expense, Álvaro and I. The club's official bank was Unicaja, who were based in Málaga but our personal bank accounts were with Banco de Sabadell and, come pay day, our wages had to go into Unicaja first, then transferred into our personal bank account, leading to a delay of about two or three days, which we didn't appreciate much. So, every time we drove past the clubs' bank, we'd have some banter and shout out, "Unicaja hijo de puta," which translated to "Unicaja, sons of bitches."

Álvaro hated playing against me in training, even though he and our other centre-back, Armando Lozano were built like monsters. Armando was the dirty one and he wasn't a player you'd mess about with – funnily enough, I hated playing against him. I don't know whether it was because we were good friends but Álvaro wouldn't go in hard when trying to tackle me – maybe he didn't want to hurt me. However, I loved playing against him because when I had the ball and was facing him, I'd skin him alive.

Six months into the season, Moreno was sacked as coach of Málaga 'B' following a poor run of results. He was a quiet guy and didn't really say much but he worked a lot with me and was always positive. His replacement was Francisco José 'Lobo' Carrasco in January 2006. From day one, I sensed Carrasco hated my guts, or at least that's the impression he gave me. In one particular game against Sevilla B, I was on the bench, which I wasn't happy about, but during the game the fans started singing my name, "Samba, Samba, Samba…" and some of the fans closest to the dugout were asking me why I wasn't playing. With 20 minutes to go, he put me on with us 2-1 up. At one point, I picked the ball up from a deep position, took on two players and shot at goal. I should have scored but the shot went wide. For the next 15 minutes, Sevilla were on top with counter-attack after counter-attack. However, the boss wasn't happy with the way we were playing so he made another substitution and, to my surprise, I saw my number being held up. I'd only been on the pitch for 20 minutes so I thought he was having a laugh. Being subbed after you've just come on as a substitute is the biggest insult to any footballer, so I really wasn't happy with his decision. What was he doing?

Apparently, he took me off because I'd missed that golden chance to seal the victory and he sacrificed a striker, me, for a defender to try and stop their counter-attacking. When the fans saw my number being held up by the fourth official, they started booing and swearing at the coach. I was thinking to myself, "Is he taking the piss or what?" My teammates were looking at me as if they felt sorry for me – they didn't want to look at my face because they knew how I was feeling. All sorts of things were going through my head while I started the long, slow walk off the pitch. I was fuming!

Then the referee told me to hurry up because I didn't want to get off the pitch, to which I replied (in Spanish), "No, I'm not going to fucking hurry up! Go on, give me a card". So he did and it was a yellow one. By that time I was seething and after been given a yellow card I said to him, "Now, I'm not coming off the pitch until I get a red card, ref." I said that for a reason because I felt insulted by being subbed after I'd only just come on, so I wanted the referee to send me off. I reluctantly decided to walk off, even though the referee refused to give me a red card and our captain, Armando stopped me and said, "We'll talk about this after the game. Just go. We all know what's going on so just go." I listened to what he said and slowly strolled off the pitch as if I had all day. The referee approached me again and shouted, "Hey Samba, hurry up, hurry up". At that point I didn't give a toss so answered him back again, "Give me a fucking red card – I don't care". I knew exactly what I was doing and, lo and behold, he finally sent me off. I then walked off the field, took my shirt off, threw it towards Carrasco and walked down the tunnel to get changed. The fans saw it and I expected them to turn their backs to me, as they do in Spain if they don't like something, but they actually started to applaud me.

Being sent off is never nice but, on that occasion, I actually wanted to be sent off, rather than being subbed, so once I'd got changed I sat in the dressing room and waited for my teammates. Towards the end of the game, I heard some jeering and I knew that Sevilla had scored an equaliser. After the final whistle blew, the players came into the changing room followed by the manager. When Carrasco saw me, he blew his top in front of everyone. I wasn't bothered about what he said and after showering I took off and went home. I immediately gave Benito a call to explain what had happened during the game. He wasn't happy with what he heard so he promised me he'd contact the people at Málaga and advised me to get away for the rest of the weekend to clear my head.

I distinctly remember after that game, Álvaro suggested we all go to Marbella for the weekend. It was a good call, and we all drove there, checked into a hotel and just spent the weekend chilling out together in one of the most expensive areas of Spain. Angerine was pregnant at the time, so the timing wasn't brilliant, but it was an amazing few days and he took care of us all the time, and we came back on the Monday, ready for training on the Tuesday.

To this day, I still keep in touch with Álvaro and Kiki nearly every day because they are top blokes and have become good friends. I can never repay people like Sergio, Álvaro and Kiki for the love they showed me.

The news of my sending off had made all the papers over the weekend and it seemed I was the talk of the town. We had a team meeting on the Tuesday and throughout the meeting I had one of the players in my ear, telling me to apologise to the manager and he was annoying me. At the end of the meeting, Carrasco asked the group if anyone had anything to say and Armando took the unprecedented step of standing up to address the manager, "Mister, I think what you did on Saturday wasn't right. We were comfortable at the back and we were attacking them. There was only 10 minutes left. It would have been fair and more respectful if you had sacrificed someone who had started the game rather than Samba. He came on as sub and you subbed him – that is disrespectful." As he was speaking, I interrupted and said, "Armando, you don't have to say all that." I then addressed Carrasco, "Mister, look, first of all I want to apologise to my team – I cost us a win. I want to play as a team. I'm sorry. I shouldn't have done that and I should have done the decent thing and come off the field when I was asked. That's all."

When all the talking had ended, Carrasco came up to me and said we needed to talk. He asked me if I was happy at the club, to which I replied honestly and in no uncertain terms, "I was happy here until you came. Why don't you like me? Is it because I'm English? Is it because I'm black? Are you saying I'm not good enough? What is it? You've been here three months and I've worked my socks off every day for you. After training sessions all the players go home, but I stay there with you and work. I'm improving week in, week out." At that point I started to cry and he looked at me and said, "Look, my formation is 4-3-3 and you want to play at the top. The type of player you are I don't think you can do a job for me." I couldn't believe he actually said that to me, "What type of player am I? I don't understand. I've played in every forward position for England so tell me where can I play in your formation?" He then said to me, "Your problem is when you don't have the ball. You don't press enough, unlike other players. You only come alive when you have the ball. I can't afford you even though you're one of the greatest, most skilful players we have at the club, but when you haven't got the ball you're a liability." I couldn't honestly disagree with him so I said, "Fair enough. All you needed to do was to tell me that and I'd have worked on my game." Carrasco then said, "I've told you now so, if you do it, you get in the team, but I need to see that." I apologised for my behaviour again and we shook hands, but those words ended up meaning little.

After that chat, I asked him to spend time with me and help me improve that side of my game. After the following training session we spent an hour working on the pressing game but the next day, he didn't bother staying on and went home straight after training, leaving me on the field alone. It was the same every day after that – he'd make up some excuse not to train with me. So much for promises, I thought. All I was asking was for my coach to help me improve.

Even after I'd apologised again for my behaviour during that chat with Carrasco and had spent hours on the training ground trying to improve my game, he still didn't play me. In fact, I didn't play again for him, unless you count bringing me off the bench for two minutes here and there, which lasted for six or seven months. It could be said I was just a 'benchwarmer' for the rest of that season. Again, I was feeling unloved and started feeling homesick once more and it was yet another low ebb in my career. It got so bad that I even started to lose interest in football altogether, merely because I wasn't playing. It is one of the most disheartening feelings to experience as a footballer, not being part of the manager's plans and having to watch from the stands or the bench as your teammates play week in, week out.

Those negative feelings had returned to haunt me yet again. That period reminded me of the time my move to Liverpool fell through, the rejection hurt me once more; however, as I approached the end of my spell at Málaga, with Angerine pregnant, all those thoughts I had in my head were reversed and I now had something to look forward to in life. It was a million miles away from football, but it was a great feeling and it resolved our immediate future.

For the rest of that season, I played catch-up and it was tough, but I still loved my time at Málaga. I felt more at home there, having spent a season in Spain already I felt more like 'one of them' and it was the best period of my domestic football career. They were a great bunch of lads, a different group to the Cádiz lads – a more young and hungry bunch, I'd say. There was great banter between us and if I was injured or I wasn't at training some of the lads would call me and say the training wasn't the same without me. It was an unbelievable atmosphere and I would go as far to say it was the best dressing room I've experienced in professional club football.

Angerine and I decided that neither of us wanted our children to be born in Spain, so it was time to go home. It had become too much for Angerine, living in Spain, not knowing anyone there (apart from me) and she wasn't happy living like that for any amount of time.

I made Harry and Cádiz aware that I wanted to go back home. Cádiz held my registration, so in theory I was still their player and because I had two years left on my contract, it had become a problem. I told them upfront that the club would be better off with the money they'd get for me if they chose to sell me.

We went home for a few days to visit family and friends in London and shortly after returning to Spain, I had a call from Dick Bate. I explained to Dick that I had two years left on my Cadiz contract and I wanted to return to England at some stage. I told him my situation at Málaga and he said he'd see what he could do to help. He said he had a good friend who was working with Ian Holloway at Plymouth Argyle, who were in the Championship at the time, so he'd have a chat with him. I didn't realise at the time but he was calling me from Malaysia where he was working on a temporary project for the Malaysian FA – that was Dick, it didn't matter where in the world he was, he'd always have time to call me. A few days later, Dick called again to tell me that Plymouth were keen on me.

It was just the news I wanted to hear and when I told Angerine she was so happy; however, I had to wait several weeks later until something concrete happened. It was as though a decision on our immediate lives had been made for us.

After they met my advisers, Cádiz decided to terminate my contract by mutual consent to give me the opportunity to find a club and they did not want to hold me back. I was a free agent again and that was the end of my Spanish adventure; it had ended as quickly as it had begun. I suppose I could have gone back to Cádiz but the opportunity never came about, besides, we were both homesick and I was bored of not playing football. Not only that, Cádiz were strapped for cash and needed the money.

So, it was, "Adiós España," after nearly two seasons. In a funny way I was sad to leave Spain because both clubs were very good to me, and the fans even more so. I enjoyed my time there and on the whole, I was happy. I still have friends at Cádiz and to this day I keep in contact with some people there. It's a very special club to me.

Chapter 5

I Just Want To Be Loved

*"I'm looking for a proper footballer and you can become
one here. Call your agent now – I'm going to sign you"*

Ian Holloway
Former Plymouth Argyle manager

After several weeks in the wilderness, Dick called again
and told me I had to go to Plymouth for a trial and if Ian
Holloway thought I could be an asset, the club would sign
me. It was my chance to show the club what I was about.

Plymouth were playing in the Championship in 2006/2007
and when Ian Holloway (Ollie) became manager, replacing
Tony Pulis, he promised the fans he'd take the club to the
Premier League. We had some really decent players, including Bojan Djordjic, Barry Hayles, Sylvan Ebanks-Blake, a very
young Scott Sinclair and I was added to bolster the attacking
options. The prospects looked good for the season ahead.

Harry had arranged my temporary accommodation in
Plymouth so all I had to do was turn up for training. I had a
choice of staying in a soulless hotel or digs in the town, so
I chose the latter. I arrived at my digs and was greeted by a
lady called Lorraine Rogers, who ran the guesthouse with
her husband, Alan. I knew from that first moment I would be
happy there. Lorraine and Alan's job, as my housekeepers, was
to look after me and take care of everything for me. I could tell
they loved looking after their guests and they wouldn't let me

do anything. I'd been taught to help around the house since the age of eight, so it came natural to me to help, so on my first day I cleared the table and washed the dishes for them. I think I surprised and impressed them because they weren't used to their guests doing the dishes. Little did I know at the time, but they must have phoned the club to tell them and it even got back to Ian Holloway.

Hearsay and stigma can be very powerful in football, so the next day one of the coaches, Des Bulpin pulled me aside and said, "Before you came here I spoke to a lot of people and what they said to me was you had a talent, but a poor attitude. Nobody could question your ability." I'd heard it all before and it was a legacy I'd inherited from Millwall – and it wasn't going away. Anyway, Des carried on, "I don't know what you're doing, whether you're doing it for pretence or doing it for show, but whatever you're doing carry on, because it's getting to the bosses that your helping out and washing the dishes." It was a strange conversation to say the least, my coach telling me to carry on washing the dishes. I took it as a positive that I was being helpful around the house, even though I was probably the only young footballer ever to wash dishes at their digs.

When I returned to the guesthouse that evening, Lorraine had bought a takeaway for us and said I didn't have to pay anything and she told me I could stay there as long as I wanted to. Happy days, I thought. I think they'd done their research on me and knew about my upbringing and my family life, and she soon considered me to be part of her family.

I'd been in Plymouth for about five days before my first game, a friendly organised by Ian Holloway, and Lorraine encouraged Alan to go and watch me play. I knew that Alan was an ex-footballer himself, having played for Portsmouth, Southend United and Cardiff City, before buying the guesthouse. I think Lorraine wanted to know if I was any good and lived up to my reputation. With everyone watching me, I scored four goals in an 8-1 win and I was doing things I didn't know I had in my locker. The best part of that day was when I got back to the guesthouse and was greeted by Lorraine, who just hugged me and said, "You were so good, Cherno." Alan came home from the game later and he said to me as one player to another, "You like drifting in from the left don't you? I like that". That was a trait of my game – I tended to come in from a wide position and take a shot at goal. Alan then gave me some more words of encouragement, "You carry on like that and you'll get far in football. You've got natural ability, for sure."

The next day the gaffer took me into his office and said to me, "I saw the game – fantastic; attitude – spot on; ability on the pitch – unbelievable; technically, I'm looking for a proper footballer and you can become one here. Call your agent now – I'm going to sign you". It was just the shot in the arm I was looking for, but he hadn't finished because he then gave me some sound advice.

He said, "I want to tell you a story. There was a player who was earning £35,000 a week for five years. After the five years, how much of that money do you think he had left?" I thought about the situation and the question and responded, "About £6m?" Ian then told me, "No, he only had ten grand left in his pocket. I can't tell you the name of that player because he's very well known but my point is you'll be earning good money here, so take my advice and save your fucking money and put it to good use."

That conversation with Ian really hit home to me and helped me understand what a short career football can be. I decided there and then that the money I'd earn would be put to good use so I discussed this with Angerine and with Harry, who knew a lot about property development, and we decided to buy a property in the Plymouth area. I had done so much travelling in my short career but we felt Plymouth was such a nice family orientated place that we wanted to bring up our family there while I still had the chance to further my football career. We all agreed that, even if we had to move again, the property would be an investment for the future. I was getting older and now had a family to think about. The club helped by giving me a relocation package and they helped find us a nice, new build home near the town.

It seemed like the right club for me and a challenge I was well up for, so I signed a two-year contract. I made my debut on 30 September 2006 as a second-half substitute against Coventry City at the Ricoh Arena and within eight minutes I'd scored my first Plymouth goal as we beat the Sky Blues 1-0.

That debut goal helped reignite my confidence and it showed what hard work can bring. I was back, or on the way back, anyway. Just before that debut goal, Des Bulpin helped me with my heading because it wasn't my best asset and the lads were dissing me about it somewhat; even Ollie was having a go, telling me I needed to get my head in there a bit more often. We were working on technique for about two weeks flat and then, lo and behold, my debut goal was a header. Thanks Des. After that, Des used to kiss my forehead every time I headed the ball – he was quite a character.

Once that goal went in, the media went mad for me; Sky came to interview me and ITV brought a film crew down to the South West to do a piece on me, where I showed off some of my skills and told them of my ambitions for Plymouth. The piece ITV did was made famous when Ollie showed off a fake bum in front of the camera – it was hilarious and a bit Gazza-esque. Wow! I was happy again and I remember sitting down, chatting to another player at the club, saying it just shows what a thin line there is between being failure and success.

Talking of Ian Holloway, I have to say here and now, he was one of the best managers I have worked under in my football career, certainly in terms of man-management, motivational skills and how he got the best out of his players. I found him very down-to-earth and very family orientated. I think his own situation at home has made him grounded and someone who knows footballers are just like anyone else, with issues at home from time-to-time. I think the players appreciated that approach and respected him for it. From the first time I met him, I looked up to him as someone who could be good for my career.

What I loved about Ollie was that he didn't try and restrict me on the pitch in terms of what I could do best; he just let me play my natural game and that went for all the other players too. He encouraged us to go and enjoy ourselves on the pitch, more than anything else. Not many people give him much credit for being a tactician, but I found Ollie very tactically aware – he was absolutely spot-on – and he used to change games by tweaking his tactics during a match. For a manager to get a team like Blackpool (no disrespect to them) promoted to the Premier League, he must have something special about him.

The first player I met when I joined the club was Sylvan Ebanks-Blake, who'd signed for Plymouth from Manchester United a few weeks before I joined the club, just before the start of the season. We hit it off straight away and he showed me around the place and made me feel wanted. I was still a little bit nervous, coming back into English football after the hard time I'd had in Spain, so I was pleased to make a strong connection so quickly.

Sylvan is a really quiet guy off the field, but on it he's an animal; he has a wicked shot on him and can bang goals in, left, right and centre. I remember during one of the first training sessions I had under Ollie, he got us to watch the movie, 'Coach Carter', which at first I thought was strange, but having watched it, I guess epitomised Ian himself. I was sitting next to Sylvan watching the movie, and he was engrossed in it and said it was very motivating. I guess it gave us both an insight into how Ollie worked and how he liked to motivate his players.

Sylvan and I soon became good friends and we'd stay around the training ground doing extra training and we'd very often socialise together. We worked hard on the field and we enjoyed every minute of it.

When I bought my property in Plymouth, I told Sylvan about how good a deal it was and he also bought a property in the same development – next door, in fact. Our families grew close as well and we'd very often be round each other's houses for dinner. For that short time we spent together, we were like brothers and I can't thank him enough for helping me settle into life at Plymouth. For a guy who was younger than me, I respect him so much for the welcome he gave me and for those great times we had. Without doubt, he was one of the main reasons I enjoyed my time there and we are still touch now. He's a really nice, down-to-earth guy and someone I will never forget.

Ian is an inspirational guy and he doesn't mess about when you've got a problem in your life either. After a game against Ipswich Town, I must have been a bit of homesick, so I told him my Mum was sick and in hospital (she wasn't) and he replied, "Well, what the fuck are you doing here then? Get in your car and drive there now and when you get there you'd better call me and tell me she's ok." So, I took his advice and drove to London in the early morning and I duly texted Ollie to tell him she was ok. In fact, he was the type of guy who would have wanted to have a chat with my Mum but as I had told a fib, I just texted him. In fact, I did that a few times during my Plymouth career but each time, he was fine with it.

Ollie is a phenomenal man. He loves his football and he loves his players. He used to advise me, not only in football terms, but in life too. He was a lovely man – a very wise and clever guy – and he'd often advise me about investments and how I should spend my money wisely. Within three months of being at Plymouth, I bought a new Mini for Angerine and we used to share it for a while.

Even though we had our new house, a new car and a family, I felt as though something was still missing and seeing the other players driving their new cars around made me feel that I wanted my own car, too. Ever since I was young, I'd always loved BMWs, so I couldn't resist it and invested in my first expensive top-of-the-range 3-Series convertible. Buying that car was contrary to the gaffer's financial advice and I don't think he was too happy when he found out I'd bought what he called a 'Zimmer'.

What Ollie saw in me when I signed for him was a shy, humble lad who just wanted to play football, but as soon as I bought the 'Zimmer' he spoke to me about it and said, "Erm, look, you shouldn't have done that – you should have waited a bit". In hindsight, he was right of course. He had given me a chance to establish myself from my two years in the wilderness of Spain and I hadn't taken his advice. I should have gone under the radar and I shouldn't have appeared flash almost as soon as I'd arrived at the club. There was no need to rush and buy that car, even though it was a beauty that I'd craved all my life. Ollie was right, and so was Fes, who had heard me bang on about my dream car for years.

Having said all that, sharing a car with my wife when the other players had flash motors meant it was probably only a matter of time before I picked up my own. I had my reasons for wanting that car and being in such a rush to get it. Number one: I was in love with BMWs – they were my cars. Number two: I had to buy it to say to myself, "I'm back." That was the mentality I had at the age of 21. It was like, "I'm back in England, back on home soil and that's what I'm driving. I'm in the Championship. I've made it again. I'm not a failure anymore". So, in my own mind I had to get that car for my own ego and to have my own status. Hindsight is a beautiful thing and I know now (and I knew then if I'm being honest) that I shouldn't have bought that particular car at that particular time, because it wasn't the right thing to do.

Ollie didn't care about egos or reputations, good or bad, so he took me on face value and we started with a clean slate.

I think he saw me as a bit of a 'project' and he thought he could be the one to help me get to where I should be. My antics off the pitch regarding the 'Zimmer' didn't help endear me to him though, and in fact subsequently soured our relationship in a way. We were still talking, but he started to question some of the decisions I was making.

Paul Wotton was the 'main man' at the club during my spell there. He was the absolute blue-eyed boy and during training sessions none of the players would dare tackle him. He'd been at the club since a boy and he seemingly had the lay of the land at the club – it seemed he could do anything he wanted. He was 'Mr Plymouth' and he was the nicest lad if you were on his side but the nastiest player you could play against.

There was one instance when he tackled me hard, I got the hump, stood up to him and said in his face, "What are you fucking doing? What did you do that for?" Immediately, everyone on that training pitch stopped and watched us having a ding-dong. They couldn't believe I'd spoken out to him. Sylvan came up to hold me back and tried to cool me down, but I reacted again, which made Paul react and we got into blows on the training pitch. The one thing about me when I was playing, either in a game or in training, was that I didn't take any nonsense from anybody, not even 'Mr Plymouth'.

Ironically, shortly after that incident Paul bought a new house and surprisingly invited me to the housewarming, along with everyone else from the club. That made me think differently about him and, from then on, I got to know him and his family well and we became good mates, though it didn't stop us having friendly banter on the training pitch from time-to-time.

There was another incident I was involved in which I wasn't proud of. I was taking part in some shooting practice during a training session against a young Hungarian 'keeper and every time I took a shot he'd save it – how dare he?! I was there for over an hour and he just kept saving every effort that went on target. I couldn't score and I was getting more and more frustrated. After the session, he started having teasing me, saying things like, "You didn't score against me, ha, ha" and some of the other lads joined in too, "You know Cherno, you couldn't score in a brothel, mate". I was getting wound up so I stupidly retaliated, "Stop it mate, you're getting on my tits, now". He just laughed and carried on having a go, so I looked at him and spat in his face.

It's not a thing I planned – it just happened as a reaction. It was a horrible thing to do – he'd got into my head but there was no excuse for that sort of behaviour.

He told his father and the next day he actually came down to the training ground to find me. Somehow he managed to get into the dressing room and spoke to the gaffer about the incident. Ollie called me in and was furious at me, "I'm fining you two weeks wages because you shouldn't be doing that. That's a kid who was making fun of you, Cherno – a kid. You're going to apologise to him." I duly apologised to the lad and his father, but that episode didn't do my relationship with Ollie any good and he put me on the bench for the next few games, which I deserved.

I'd shot myself in the foot once again because that incident signalled the beginning of a month-long loan move to, of all places, Wrexham, in the early part of 2007. I didn't know at the time, but the intention was for me to be loaned out for two months to get game-time, however I ended up only playing three times for them – and hated every minute of my time there. The manager Brian Kerr played me on the wing and I didn't want to play there – in fact I didn't want to be in Wrexham at all. For my last game, away at Grimsby, Brian put me on the bench so I questioned his decision. He'd already decided he wanted to try something different, to which I said, "Are you trying to take the piss? League Two? I've been playing up front in the Championship and now you're telling me I can't play up front in League Two? I don't want to be here. I want to terminate my loan." I was bored and lonely the whole time and, to make matters worse, I was stuck in a dismal hotel with another player who was on loan from Stoke. It was a pretty bad period in my life, one which I'd like to forget, and I was that fed up and embarrassed that I didn't even allow Fes to come and visit – he always visited wherever I was playing, until I went to Wrexham. The club terminated my loan deal and I went back to Plymouth with my tail between my legs.

A few things I did had upset Wrexham, not all were football-related, and everything was reported back to Ian Holloway at my parent club. Unsurprisingly, Ollie froze me out after that and I ended up being benched for months, even though I was training hard and trying to make a good impression. Ollie approached me at one stage and told me he was going to put me on the transfer list, "Look, speak to your agent to find another club. You can train with us but you're not going to play." After hearing that I knew where I stood, but I carried on training hard and I couldn't understand why he wasn't seeing what I was doing in training – I was banging goals in left, right and centre. He continued to freeze me out until one day he stopped me and said, "Look, this is how it is. We're going on a pre-season training camp in Austria – I'm not going to take you so by the time we return, I expect you to have found a new club."

There was no shortage of goal scorers at the club, so when they came back from Austria, he would have no option but to leave me on the transfer list. I didn't find a new club, so I carried on training and giving it my all to hopefully convince him to give me another chance.

Suddenly, two or three months in to the new season, Ollie dropped a big bombshell on the club and on my own future. Following press speculation, he handed in his resignation to the Plymouth board; after some wrangling over his contract and having agreed a compensation package for his services, he was announced in a press conference as the new Leicester

City manager in late November 2007. I owed a lot to Ollie as he had educated me and widened my knowledge of the game, but I'd failed to repay his faith in me and I had let him down on several occasions.

Paul Sturrock took over as our manager shortly after Ollie left. He'd actually been Plymouth manager before, leading the club to two promotions before leaving for Southampton in 2004. Lorraine let me into the secret shortly before he was announced to the media – I knew they had a connection with Paul Sturrock as he stayed there when he first joined the club as a manager, but I didn't realise they were still in touch with him. Lorraine told me I'd be ok with Paul as manager so I started to get my hopes up that I'd get a run in the side and she promised to have a word with Paul about me.

I was initially happy with his appointment, but it soon became obvious that he already had an idea of how he wanted his team to play football and that he didn't like pacey, technical players like me. All he wanted were grafters, so I would struggle to play in his team, but all I wanted was to be given a chance.

On his first day at the club we had a trial game where he put me on the right wing and I did really well, even though I hated playing there. If you were an outsider watching that game, you'd have thought I was 'the next big thing'. However, in the second-half I wasn't getting the ball and, thinking I was doing the right thing, I started drifting onto the left wing and all over the pitch to try and get the ball. Even though I enjoyed myself on the pitch, Sturrock said he wasn't looking for that and after the game he told me I "lacked discipline".

As the right-winger in the game, he said he'd wanted me to stay up top and not drift from left to right "like Ronaldo or whoever you think you are". He went on, "It's not going to work in my team. Looking at what you did in that test game, you're going to be unreliable because you'll get frustrated if you tuck in there without getting the ball and you're going to lose the shape of the side". He was very a disciplined and fairly old school manager who liked his players to have their own jobs on the pitch.

After that trial game, I knew my days were numbered and it wasn't a surprise when he told me I wasn't part of his plans and he was going to put me on the transfer list. That killed me instantly because I'd bought a house in the area and we were settling down as a family. The fans loved me and I didn't want to leave Plymouth but Sturrock gave me no option. I was absolutely devastated.

Although I wasn't living with Lorraine and Alan any more, I used to bump into them before or after each home game. When I told them the news Sturrock didn't want me, they didn't believe me at first – they were shocked and thought I was messing about. Again, as Lorraine knew him so well she promised to speak to Sturrock in person to see if I had upset him in any way, which she did, but nothing happened and I remained on the transfer list.

After a couple of weeks, the manager just told me outright that I needed to leave and I should find another club as soon as possible. I took the news in good spirit and I didn't make a fuss or beg him – I'm not that type of person. He had already made it clear he didn't fancy me as a player and there was nothing anyone could do to change his mind. I didn't need to grovel to him. He said his piece and that was the end of that.

Regrettably, I started to avoid Lorraine and Alan, for what reason I don't know and can't explain, other than I maybe felt I had let them down in some way. Those lovely people touched my heart and proved very influential in my life. That avoidance has lasted nearly ten years and I've not spoken to either of them since, which saddens me so much because it doesn't show the real me. I know I should have called them up but my own stubbornness stopped me from even doing that. It's like I've betrayed them and they didn't deserve that. I hope one day I can rectify it and we can meet up once more, then I will sit down and explain to them why they have not had a call from me, because they are special people.

I didn't know at the time, but I later found out that I had a clause built into my Plymouth contract that stated I would get a new contract with a higher salary after I'd played 20 games. I believe these clauses are ploys used by agents to make sure their players are rewarded when they play a certain number of games for a club. However, in my case, it may have worked against me as I was having trouble getting playing time and the club began to struggle financially during my second season. As I approached my 19th game, I was left out of the team, maybe because of that clause in my contract, but who knows?

I do believe it held me back in my Plymouth career and I ultimately played just 19 games for the club, scoring that single debut goal. Looking back, I don't feel I was given a fair chance in the first team and I think that explains my poor goal return.

Obviously, Paul would have known about my clause – whether or not that affected his decision to keep me on the transfer list, I don't know. Clauses in players' contracts can work for or against the player, depending upon the situation at the club but, for me, it worked out badly. Unfortunately, those sort of clauses in contracts still exist in football and in my opinion they are bad for the game and bad for the players, especially when it doesn't work out.

Picking up a trophy at
Wembley Stadium during
Primary school years

Mum and I

Posing in the bedroom

Mum, Dad and I at first trials for
England under 15's at Lilleshall

South London District Team featuring Anton
Ferdinand, James Cheesman & Ben Watson

South London District Team featuring Anton
Ferdinand, James Cheesman & Ben Watson

England under 16's in Brazil

England under 17's in Portugal

England under 17's: Dinner time with Glen Johnson

England under 16's in Brazil

Picking up 'Best Player of the Year' at Mottingham Youth FC

Mottingham Youth FC

England under 16's with Jamie Cade

At Liverpool FC with Robbie Fowler and John
Welsh at the height of the negotiations

Posing in the living room

England under 16's at the Maracana Stadium in Brazil

SENSATIONAL SAMBA: The schoolboy goal machine has already been compared to Arsenal's Kanu and Liverpool striker Emile Heskey

School days at St Joseph's Academy

Signing my first professional contract with Millwall
FC alongside Mum, Dad, Harry and Mick Beard

During the Liverpool FC negotiations

My cousin Omar, my brother Baboucarr (Lause) and I

Some of my England caps

England under 17's: After semi final loss to
France in the European Championships

England under 17's with Chris Eagles

In action for England at the European Championships 2001

England under 17's with Scott Carson

African Cup of Nations qualifier: Gambia vs Senegal....we drew 1-1

Alvaro Silva and I at Malaga FC

England under 17's squad

Modelling whilst Cadiz FC in Spain

Fes settling my nerves on my wedding day!

My soulmate, Angerine and I

In action for FC Haka in Finland

In action for FK Tonsberg in Norway

On my wedding day with family

Playing for Malaga FC

My younger brother, Malick and I

African Cup of Nations qualifier: Gambia vs Senegal

Fes and I at the 'Football for Peace' charity event

Modelling whilst Cadiz FC in Spain

Chilling with the Mrs

Harry Redknapp and I: Wish I got to play for him!

Matt and Nick Bate: The sons of my 'Football Father', Dick Bate

Coaching at Tottenham Hotspur FC

Modelling for my sister's clothing line,
www.instagram.com/colourmej

Special invitation for the family and I at Plymouth

At the shoot for the Football Manager 2017 advert

Frank Lampard, Graeme Le Saux and I on our A license course

Coaching under 9's

My football academy in Gambia

My football club in Gambia, Samger FC

Chapter 6

The Globetrotter

"You want me to run? I'm a footballer, not an athlete."

I continued to train hard at Plymouth, even after Paul Sturrock had told me I wouldn't be part of his plans. I just didn't suit his style of football, which was fair enough so I had to find another club.

For weeks, there was no interest from any other club but then, out of the blue, San Jose Earthquakes from the MLS came in for me and it seemed America beckoned.

It was an exciting prospect and I was invited to go to San Jose to talk to the club so, of course, I wasn't going to turn down the opportunity to speak to them. I liked what I saw there and, after several conversations, the club offered me a four-year contract; however, there was a big sticking point. The way transfers worked in the MLS was different to how they worked in Europe. Their clubs only had one 'marquee player' and all the rest of the players the club wanted to sign had three months to prove they were good enough. If, after that period you didn't convince them you were worth a contract, the club would let you go. In theory it's kind of like a probationary period but it seemed like a fair enough system and it's the way most commercial companies' work.

However, I thought about the consequences of the system for me and decided I could have been shooting myself in the foot if I had accepted it. It wasn't as if I was going to another club in Europe; America is a different continent and there is a totally different approach to the game. I was probably being stubborn, but something didn't sit right with me. I could have played brilliantly for two months but then played terrible for the final month and found myself on the first plane back to London.

I told San Jose, nicely, thanks but no thanks – I wasn't interested. My life would have been on hold for that period. No chance!

Wow, what had I done? I'd just turned down a four-year contract in San Jose, California. I would have loved the lifestyle but the salary wasn't great, compared to what I could have earned in England. Had I made the biggest mistake of my career? Maybe, but we'll never know now.

Even though I'd turned them down, San Jose asked me to stay and train with them for a month to prove my fitness, if nothing else. I took that opportunity and it proved to be an expensive month. For those four weeks, I spent money like there was no tomorrow – I blew over US$10,000 on utter rubbish, although I did spend plenty in the Nike store. I hooked up with another lad who was at the club, Kei Kamara, who's still playing at the top level in the MLS. Spending was the only thing that kept me happy during those weeks away. Kei also took me out to some of the top nightclubs and we met some world-famous stars, including an up-and-coming Rihanna.

I returned home – back to reality and back to Plymouth, where I still had a year left on my contract. As they had no plans for me, I asked the club to pay my contract up, which I was entitled to do. It was finally agreed that I'd leave Plymouth 'by mutual agreement' and I left with 80% of my contract paid up.

I was feeling down again and unwanted so, needless to say, I also blew my payday from Plymouth. I hadn't felt like that for quite some time, but I'd learned lessons from my time at Cádiz and I knew I wouldn't do anything stupid. The only thing that would cheer me up was to spend my money, which seemed very shallow, I know, but it was the way I was feeling at that time in my life.

****

At the age of 22, I was a free agent and yet again looking for another club. I was training here and there at clubs like Southend and Wycombe, just to keep my fitness up. Then one day, a foreign agent called me out of the blue and asked if I'd be interested in playing football in Finland; FC Haka were keen to speak to me. I'd never heard of FC Haka and didn't even realise the Finns knew how to play football. All I knew about Finland was how cold it was; however, I later found out that FC Haka were actually one of the most successful clubs in the country.

I showed some initial interest and asked the agent if he could get FC Haka to book me a ticket to fly over there and meet the club's representatives. He seemed a bit taken aback by that request but he promised to get back to me. A few days later, the agent called me to say the club had agreed to book my ticket to fly to Helsinki. I ended up staying there for one week, but the club were having money problems and when they initially offered me a deal, I insisted they would need to up their offer as I could have got more playing for a lower league team in England. During the week there, I trained with the club and the manager Olli Huttunen, a former Finland international goalkeeper, who got to know me and started to like me as a player.

Surprisingly, there was another African boy there called Abdullahi Ishaka who was training with the club in the hope of getting a deal. I asked Abdullahi if he was going to sign and he suggested he'd only sign if I did – we both had nowhere else to go, if I'm honest, so when the club upped their offer to me, we both agreed 18-month deals in 2008. Olli wanted both of us to sign and thought we'd be very good additions to the squad.

So, I'd got a deal to play football in a very unfashionable place and, I'm sorry to say, I really didn't like Finland one bit. Although I'm sure the majority of people in Finland are lovely, the experiences I had with some people there made me dislike the country. Olli was a good guy and I liked some of the people at the club, but I didn't like the weather or the town. It seemed to snow all year round – it became a very bad decision for me. It was horrible! It was probably the worse time I have had as a footballer; so bad that I told my wife and Fes not to come and visit me as I'd come home as often as I could to see them. It was worse than being at Wrexham, which was saying a lot. If Abdullahi wasn't there, I doubt I could have lasted more than a week, that's for sure.

The worse part of being there was the boredom – there was literally nothing to do. We lived in a town called Valkeakoski, three hours from Helsinki. Being a footballer in a small town, I'd expect people to recognise me, but nobody knew who I was. It was the first time I'd come across that and I found it strange that nobody in the town seemed to be interested in football at all.

From a footballing perspective, Finland wasn't exactly fashionable and that was reflected in the attendances we had – I think the stadium only held 3,500 and it was rarely full. Being a cold climate most of the time, it was the only place I'd ever played football and didn't sweat – I'd play for 45 or 90 minutes but when I finished playing I felt as though I could have played again. The pace of the game was slow and physically, it wasn't hard – I didn't have to push myself that much.

There was only one game which sticks out and that was against HJK Helsinki; and even then it was only because they had a fellow Gambian playing for them. His name was

Dawda Bah and in fact, he's still playing in Finland today – he deserves a medal for playing in that league for 13 years.

The game was actually very interesting and it drew a decent crowd. It was the only time during my stay in Finland that there was a capacity crowd; the game was tense and the atmosphere was electrifying. We had to be on top form that day and, although I didn't score, I hit the bar twice and I had the best game in a Haka shirt. I remember that game for two reasons. I'd just come back from playing for Gambia, along with Dawda, and secondly I'd been dropped from the Haka first team for the previous game so I had a point to prove to the manager, the club and the fans. I bullied their defence that day, running the channels and playing my natural game. I felt good about myself for the first time in Finland.

I disliked being in Finland so much that I constantly found excuses to stay away from the place. The first time I was called up to play for the Gambian national side against Liberia, I had planned to be away for one week as Haka and had a game and they were really counting on me to come back in time to play. However, I told the club that I needed to be away for two weeks then went to London for the second week instead of going back to Finland. In fact, every time I got called up subsequently, I made up an excuse not to go back after the first week away. Even worse, I once told the club that I had been called up for international duty even when there was no international match for Gambia, just to get the heck out of that place for two weeks. It wasn't the best thing I'd ever done in my life, but I had to do something just to stay away.

At first, the club put me up in a hotel and kept telling me that my flat "would be ready soon", but that went on for weeks and weeks and on top of that, the hotel constantly moved me, which meant I never settled down. It was doing my head in and it made me dislike the country even more. I couldn't even complain because hardly anyone in the hotel spoke English. It was the only place I'd lived in where I didn't have all my clothes at my disposal and it felt like I was going there to work for a few weeks at a time, then going home for a few days to get more clothes.

There were two main things that got on my nerves while I was in Finland; the fact hardly anyone spoke English and a large majority of the people I came into contact with were, in my opinion, racist – and that includes the players.

That's a bold statement, but in my opinion, it was a correct deduction at the time. My perception of Finland as a country and the people I met is that the majority of the people where I was staying were ignorant of the minority groups who live there, including Muslims. In fact, I believe most of my own teammates had racist tendencies too and that's the saddest part of all.

It seems that everywhere I go in the world, I stand out for some reason, whether good or bad. I'm always lively in the dressing room and at Haka I was the chirpy one, but their mentality was totally different. I don't think they appreciated my sense of humour and my happiness so I eventually started to wind them up and they must have thought I was a right prick. That knocked me off my stride a bit because I was used to going to training in a good mood and seeing the rest of the lads smiling and happy, but at Haka, it was as though someone had died every day.

It was so depressing going into training – no one seemed to want to be there, but I'd go in happy and shout out, "Morning Olli, morning guys," at the top of my voice in an attempt to get a response, yet nobody looked at me. Eventually, it got to me until one day I finally lost it. I went into training my usual happy self and again I had no response, so I just said, "Fuck you all then!" You could have heard a pin drop, but as soon as I'd got that out of my system, I went to my locker and started to get changed. Obviously, I got into a spot of trouble for that outburst and the manager called me into his office for a chat.

I was still wound up and I let it be known what I thought of the club. I said something derogatory, but he didn't understand what I was talking about. I began to start laughing and so did Olli. When I explained to him, Olli laughed and just said, "You are something else, Cherno, now go and get changed".

After that episode, I decided to keep myself a bit more reserved and stopped being so chirpy and chatty. Fortunately, there was a Scottish lad called Brian Gilmour who came to the club after me and he too couldn't get to grips with the set up at Haka, so he, Abdullahi and myself used to stick together. It was a horrible atmosphere and not healthy for a football team to have these splits in the camp. At first, it was so bad that none of the local lads would pass to me and they would make it hard for me to get the ball – and they all knew I was better than them, so I think they did it on purpose. The players were very timid and, in a way, I think they were fearful of me for some reason.

Ironically, towards the end of my stay in Finland, the lads actually started to warm to me and I began to warm to them. It was strange because, after nearly 18 months of frosty relations, it all changed and I remember one of them made the effort to have a laugh with me, which encouraged some of the others to start joining in from then on.

For me though, it had gone on too long and I was so fed up that I had made up my mind to leave. I don't know what it was with the people I met in Finland – they just seemed cold and it took a long time to break the ice with them.

God knows how I lasted 18 months there! I had nowhere else to go and I was in a state of limbo, so I just stuck with it until I finally said, "No more." I called the chairman one day to tell him I wanted to go back to England; however, as I had six or eight months left on my contract, the club had to pay me off. The club was going through a tough time financially and the chairman told me they couldn't pay me, which got my back up a bit. After a few days, the club offered to pay me two months' salary, which I turned down and made an ultimatum, which included the club paying me in instalments over an eight-month period. The alternative was for the club to pay me in full or I'd stay and see out my contract, which would have had a negative effect on the team and on me.

The club had paid for a dozen or so flights during my time there and actually asked me to pay them back, so I agreed but only when I'd received my last pay cheque. It was a situation I'd never found myself in before. Here I was, in a position of power making demands to a club that clearly couldn't afford to pay me. Looking back, the whole 18 months at Haka was a nightmare and the way I handled the situation wasn't something I was proud of, but we all learn by our mistakes, which seemed to be the theme of my life back then.

I returned to London and, as requested, the club duly paid me on the 27th of each month for eight months. While I was back home, I had time on my hands to enjoy my life, but I was without a club. I continued to look for opportunities during those eight months and I think I went to train at Norwich and Portsmouth, among others.

While I was in dispute with Haka, an opportunity arose through an agent called Ambrose Mendy, who used to be Nigel Benn's agent. I knew Ambrose from a long time ago and we met up again while I was on international duty for Gambia. He told me that Blackburn Rovers were interested in talking to me and he set up a trial and a meeting with their manager, Paul Ince. I ended up being there for two or three weeks and I impressed Blackburn so much that they wanted to take me on; however, they didn't want to pay the £50,000 fee that Haka wanted so, unsurprisingly, the deal didn't happen.

In football, as in normal life, things can happen quickly and sometimes unexpectedly. While I was training with Blackburn in November 2008, I met another agent called Sascha

Empacher, who incidentally now has some of Europe's top footballers in his camp. He must have been watching me train because he approached me one day while I was in the restaurant at the training ground. He complimented me on my technical ability and told me he was hoping to do a deal for one of his players, the Egyptian international, Ahmed Elmohamady, who was also at Blackburn for a five-day trial. As it turned out, that deal fell through. While we were talking he gave me his business card and we went our separate ways, until weeks later when I was sitting at home relaxing and I decided to call Sascha in the hope of him finding me a club.

True to his word, Sascha started hunting for a suitable opportunity for me. The first place he took me to was Germany and a Bundesliga club called Arminia Bielefeld. That turned out to be a bit of a disaster because the person who was meant to collect me from the airport up didn't turn up, so I missed the trial. I didn't even go to the club to meet the manager because Sascha had booked me on a plane straight back to London.

After that false start, Sascha and I stayed in touch and one day he called me up with some more positive news. At that time, all I was interested in, if I'm being perfectly honest, was the money. Sascha offered me the chance to go and play in Israel and the money on offer was pretty good so I agreed. However, I didn't hear back from Sascha, so I didn't even get to Israel.

Now, here's the interesting part. Unbeknown to me, Sascha arranged for another agent to call me one day out of the blue and offer me the opportunity to go to Iran of all places. Due to the political climate in that country, both Fes and I were nervous about the idea of me going to the Middle East. Once I'd agreed the verbal contract, the club then sent me the written version and it was staggering. The figures quoted were mind boggling – a seven-figure contract. It was serious cash but I thought they'd got the figures wrong. 'Happy days', I thought, and it seemed too good to be true. The agent gave me instructions about what I'd have to do regarding my visa and such like, so I went away and got it all stamped.

I flew off to Tehran, where I was picked up from the airport and dropped off at a nice hotel. The next day, I went to train at the club – so far, so good. However, after training, the club's officials wanted me to sign the contract, which I was happy to do, and I promised I'd sign the next day.

Here's the kicker – the contract they presented to me was totally different to the contract they had sent me before I arrived. In fact, it was so different that I thought they'd got my contract mixed up with someone else's because the copy they handed me stated a salary of £3,000 a month, compared to the one I had verbally agreed to for £1m a year. "How can this be?" I thought. There must have been some mistake, surely? The club's representatives weren't having any of it and ushered me to sign the wrong contract and tried to make me believe it was the correct one. Of course, I refused to sign and the meeting broke up without agreement and I returned to the hotel. I'd been misled big time! As you can imagine, I wasn't happy.

When I got back to the hotel, I phoned the agent and told him what had happened and insisted he get me out of the country as soon as possible as there was no way I was going to sign that contract. Not thinking clearly, I'd forgotten that the hotel had taken my passport when I checked in, but when I asked for it back they refused to give it to me. I was beginning to think it was a wind up or something and started to panic. I was a black man in an Arab country – I stuck out like a sore thumb and I was being held to ransom in a hotel and a country I wanted to leave. It felt like I'd been kidnapped and I was beginning to think the worst – that I wouldn't get out of the country alive, especially after having seen someone getting a public whipping by the authorities in the streets of Tehran that very day.

Anyway, the hotel explained that in order for me to get my passport back, I had to ask the people who had brought me there (the club) to write a letter. I knew there was no way they would write a letter so I declined that one. I had no one to talk to or fall back on and my hotel bill was increasing by the day as I was calling home from the hotel. I was confused, angry and afraid. I kept thinking, "What the fuck am I going to do?"

Not knowing the city, I decided to Google 'British Embassy in Tehran' to find directions and it proved a good call because I managed to get myself there unscathed. However, during that journey to the Embassy, I saw more horrific scenes in the streets and all I wanted to do was to go back home to a civilised country. Once I reached the embassy, I explained the situation to the official and she reiterated the fact that the people who brought me there had to write a letter to allow me out of the country – apparently, it was standard procedure. She told me to stay at the embassy building while they sorted it out.

While I was waiting for them to sort it, the agent who had arranged the deal called me to say he'd somehow got my passport back after all. The embassy advisor warned me about going back to the hotel as she thought it could be a trap and anything could happen – I was in a volatile country after all. At that point I began to shake like a leaf – was it real or was I dreaming it? I didn't really know the agent, but I trusted him enough to believe he had my passport, so I told the embassy I was going back to the hotel against their advice. Luckily enough, he had my passport and we headed back to the airport, at last.

I was beginning to think the nightmare was coming to a positive conclusion as I arrived at the airport safely, but I soon realised at the check-in counter that it was only just beginning. It was just my luck that the only flight to London that day was full, so I couldn't board it. Again, I thought the worst and I just wanted to get the hell out of the place. The agent reassured me he'd sort it so he went back to the check-in counter in the hope of somehow getting me on the flight after all. Fortunately, he came back and told me the airline had dropped an unlucky passenger off the flight and replaced them with me. I don't know what he said to the check-in girl, but it worked.

I boarded the flight and didn't say a word until the plane landed at Heathrow. It was only then that I felt I'd escaped, but how wrong I was; just as I was beginning to relax, I was stopped at customs. They had noticed where I'd arrived from, which had obviously sparked some kind of alert, and the guy questioned me as though I was a terrorist. I'd only been there one or two days, yet he asked all sorts of questions for over an hour. To be fair, my passport at the time was damaged as I'd travelled a lot with it and it looked a bit dodgy. I called Harry and explained what had happened and asked him to pick me up, but I was beginning to get a bit het up and I suddenly lost my temper with the customs guy and started shouting at him.

The police were called in to calm me down and it was at that point I used the most famous cliché of all, "Do you know who the fuck I am?" I was getting mad and talking utter crap and the police officer advised me to calm down or I'd be arrested. The policeman explained that it was standard practice for customs to randomly detain people who arrived from certain Arab countries. It was then I told him that I'd played football for England. Funnily enough, he didn't recognise me but a female officer did and she told her colleague, "Oh, my boy used to play Championship Manager and I think that's Cherno Samba." She then approached me and asked if my name was Cherno Samba and I replied abruptly, "Yes it is." Then someone else piped up and said, "Yes he is a football player and my son also plays him on Championship Manager."

I began to calm down a bit and everyone started to apologise for the inconvenience – I also apologised for my behaviour but told them that I was going to make a complaint against UK Customs, as the way I'd been treated was bang out of order. In fairness, they were only doing their job and before I left I agreed to have some photos taken with the officers and we kissed and made up. Really, it was hilarious how it had ended up.

As for going to Iran – I told myself I'd never go there again – not even for a million pounds!

Weeks later, during the winter of 2009/2010, I was still without a club and Sascha called me up again to ask if I fancied playing in Greece. I immediately jumped at the chance. However, like with most things, there was a 'but' and this time it was the amount of money the Greek 2nd Division club, Panetolikos were offering. However, the package came with a house and no bills to pay. I wasn't training anywhere and was at a loose end at the time, but I called Sascha back and declined unless the club upped their offer. It was obvious the club were desperate to sign me, plus the transfer window was about to close, so I played on that. Sascha knew what I was up to and he thought I was being very smart.

Even though the club claimed each offer was "the last offer" they kept making several more. Throughout the process, Sascha didn't think he could get the club to increase any more, but they repeatedly did – and I knew they would until it reached a certain figure that was always going to be my end point. However, not everything was clear. The final offer was very lucrative but at no time did either of us say what currency we were talking about – Euros or GBP. So, before I signed anything I had to make it clear to Sascha that I was, in fact, talking in terms of GBP so the figure was, shall we say, extremely generous. Sascha laughed and called me a "smart fucker". He must have been totally fed up with me because he had to go back one more time and confirm that I wanted more, but I told him if he got that agreed, I'd be on the plane immediately. Guess what? Panetolikos agreed on the amount and the currency. I'd just played a blinder and basically negotiated my own deal.

I was on my way to Greece and I couldn't wait to get some sun on my back and start another new chapter. Once I arrived at the club I signed the paperwork on a two-year contract without any problems.

It couldn't have been more of a contrast to Finland. The club was based in Agrinio in Western Greece. Being in the Mediterranean, the food was tremendous and the weather was hot and sunny. However, not everything was good. Although the players were friendly, the manager wasn't. Sometimes, what happens in European football is that the owners choose and buy the players, not the manager, which usually means that if the owner buys you, but the manager doesn't want you, you're basically screwed. On the flipside, if the manager buys you and it's the owner who doesn't fancy you, you're also screwed. The win-win scenario is where both the manager and owner like you, but that doesn't happen very often. In my case, the owner wanted me to sell shirts, but the manager Giannis Dalakouras didn't, so I was onto a loser from day one.

I could tell from the start that Panetolikos was a professional club and they did things in the right way. There were some really decent players there and what I liked about the club was that they tended to humble their players in a way our clubs have long since stopped doing. For example, I had to wash my own shirts and training gear. Can you imagine if any of our Premier League players had to do that?

Unfortunately, my stay in Greece was short-lived. I had an injury to my ankle and my recovery was taking too long, so they lost patience with me and terminated my contract after only six months. I'd only played a few games for them but I understood their stance – I was injured for such a long time and they were paying me handsomely, so the club was losing out.

If I recall, it was only when the club had torn up my contract that I began to consider my options after I retired from football. I had so much time on my hands as I wasn't playing, so my thoughts turned to my life after football. At the age of 26, I knew I wanted to either become a coach or go into media work within football. However, I still felt I had a job to do for some club until that day came and I was desperate to kick-start my career once more.

I was without a club again and training by myself. Once more, I was feeling down and was running out of options, running out of time and falling out of love with the game. I wasn't getting any younger and I felt like I wanted to just pack it all in once and for all. I'd been to several clubs abroad over a number of years trying to prove myself, but all I wanted was for a club to give me the chance of a decent run in the first team. I'd had trials at a number of English clubs like Nottingham Forest and Blackburn Rovers in the previous few years and I was thinking "I can't do this anymore..."

I'd even been to Dubai a couple of times in the hope of finding a club there. I loved the place but there was a hitch in that each club was only allowed a maximum of three overseas players. I was constantly being told that a certain club wanted to sign me, but they couldn't at that time for whatever reason. The money the clubs were offering was staggering so the chance to play there appealed to me greatly, but it was far from being a done deal.

While I was waiting for the Dubai deal to materialise, I was training in London on my own in the hope of something crop-ping up in the near future. The first club to show some inter-est were Dagenham & Redbridge, where my objective was to train with the club in order to keep myself in shape, but to them, I was a trialist. In my head I had no real intention of wanting to play for Dagenham as I was focused on a big contract in the Gulf; however, I was killing it in my trials and they thought I was 'the next big thing'. How many times had I heard that? Guess what? They offered me a contract, but that wasn't in the plan.

****

It was sometime during 2012 that my first cousin Yusupha, who lived in Norway, contacted me about an opportunity to play for a 2nd Division club called FK Tønsberg. He was in a barber's shop, of all places, talking to a guy who just happened to be a football agent, when he mentioned my name and said I didn't have a club. Right there and then, Yusupha called me up and put the agent on the phone to speak to me. He came straight out with it. "Do you fancy playing in Norway?" It was as simple as that. So, having nothing to lose, I said, "Ok". We agreed to talk again and that was it. Yusupha was excited at the prospect of me playing in Norway and told me the agent, whose name was Arthur, would sort something out for me.

Arthur used to be a footballer and had played with the manager of FK Tønsberg, Geir Midgsian in the past so he put me in touch with him and we spoke at length. Tønsberg really needed a player like me so the manager was very excited about signing me. The next time I spoke to Geir, he asked me when he could book my flight. We hadn't even spoken about money or contracts – he was that keen to get me to Norway – but I wanted to know how much they were going to offer me before I agreed to fly out there. However, he assured me the club would look after me in terms of money, so I agreed to fly to Oslo on that basis.

After my first training session at Tønsberg, I was asked to read the contract the club had prepared, which was lucrative and included a house, bills and car. Considering Tønsberg was a small, family club in the Norwegian 2nd Division and newly formed, it was a huge package for them to splash out on a player approaching the end of his career. However, I took one look at the contract and turned it down and said I wanted more. Even though my first impressions of the club and the city were good, I felt I'd been 'sold a kipper' by Arthur. I'd made my mind up that I wanted to sign because I had a good feeling about the city, being in a really nice part of southern Norway and because my cousin lived there; but the money was never mentioned before I'd agreed to fly out and it had become a stumbling block.

Like most small clubs, they had a budget regarding wages but they told me I'd be the highest paid player, not only in the club, but the whole league. I thought the manager was having a laugh, but I went away and did some research and found out it was true. We left it for a few hours while he went away to see if he could raise some more finance and, lo and behold, he did just that. He had found two sponsors to fund part of my package, while the club paid for the other part. I agreed to the deal and was asked to come to the ground the next day to sign the contract.

Something stood out about the manager's words to me when I signed my contract. He said he could get me back to where I belonged and that, in time, he believed and hoped an English club would come in for me. I think he said that to cover himself and he suggested that I had a buy-out clause put into my contract. In my own head, I didn't think anyone would come in for me, but I went along with it and was happy that he thought so much of my talent to do that for me.

I settled in really easily at the club and it wasn't long before I was in the team and scored in my first game. I loved my time there, playing week in, week out. I was the best-paid player in the league and the main man and I found myself taking the free kicks, corners and penalties. – I had licence to do anything I wanted to do on the football pitch. The club really looked after me. One time, the manager took me off and he shook my hand as I left the pitch, but I told him in no uncertain terms, "Don't fucking take me off again." I hated being subbed and he apologised and didn't substitute me again.

By the fourth or fifth game, the manager told me that scouts from Charlton had come to watch me and in fact had spoken to the club about me. The scouts told the club they were destined to sign me, having been close to signing me before, and said they were interested in me again. Little did I know, but Tønsberg were facing a financial crisis at the time. The alarm bells started ringing and I began to worry about my immediate future. The manager eventually spoke to me about the club's situation and they asked me what they should do, so I suggested they pay my contract off. There was nothing else to talk about – it was normal football practice in those situations. The club couldn't afford to keep me on my existing contract so they gave me what I wanted. Sadly, the club soon went into administration after that. In fact, that was in 2010 and they haven't recovered since.

There weren't many highlights of my time in Norway, except the friendship I had with two players called Mathias Eriksen and Fredrick Karlsen. Both lads were very welcoming and helped me out a lot during my time at Tønsberg. They would help me with anything I needed, at any time. They used to drive me around, to and from training, to the gym and even to pick up my shopping in the town. I can't thank them enough because without those two I honestly don't know how I would have coped.

I still have a love for that club because of the way they looked after me in the short time I was there. I had the freedom of the pitch and I played some good football, even though we played on Astro-Turf.

****

By the age of 27, opportunities were beginning to dry up. In July 2011, I joined English Conference side Forest Green Rovers on trial and played in a game against Bristol City; however, I failed to earn a contract. Things looked grim and I faced the prospect of not even being able to get into a Conference team.

During that tough period, I met an ex-pro called Mel Eves, the ex-Wolves left-sided forward from the 1970s and 1980s. He was an agent at the time and he contacted me to say how he was going to "take me back to the top". Looking at his CV, he'd actually represented some top players, including the likes of Enzo Maresca, Benito Carbone, Fabrizio Ravanelli, Robert Earnshaw and Gareth McAuley, so he had a good profile. He invited Fes and I to his office in Shepherd's Bush, and I have to say it was a pretty weird experience. He gave me the old spiel about what he was going to do for me, which was to effectively restart my career at a lower level club if I wanted to get back to the top. He was building me up and I thought it was cool and went along with it. I initially thought it made sense and as I hadn't anything going on at the time, I agreed to go along with his advice. We left his office quite optimistic and positive for the future and with the hope I'd found someone to nurture me back to the big-time. Mel 'talked-the-talk' pretty well and had done a good sales pitch on me. He had convinced us and we were thinking, "He's the guy."

A few days after our initial meeting in West London, Mel invited me to come up to Birmingham to undertake some training. Fes and I agreed to go to an indoor athletics facility in Birmingham, not really knowing what he wanted me to do. When we got there, I noticed there was a football pitch and an athletics track in the facility, and a lad being instructed by his coach and training alone on the track. It turned out that the athlete was one of the best young British sprinters around. We then met Mel, who told me to get my kit on and start training. I had no idea what he had in store for me, maybe some shooting or a five-a-side, but when I came back in my football kit, Mel told me he wanted to see me run, as I needed to work on the 'explosive side' of my game.

I thought to myself, "You want me to run? I'm a footballer, not an athlete." Basically, he'd got me up to Birmingham to undergo an athletics session. I soon realised Mel hadn't seen me play football before and I began to think, "What am I doing here? I don't get it". I spent the next hour sprinting up and down the track with this professional athlete and, to be fair, I was keeping up with a lad who could probably do 100 metres in less than 10 seconds. Although the kid was impressive, I was thinking to myself, "If I can keep up with Britain's number two sprinter, we're in trouble". It was all very odd for a footballer to prove his fitness by doing short, sharp sprints for an hour – even the athlete I was training with thought the whole thing was bizarre. Mel watched from the sidelines and asked me to repeat what I'd done for the past hour. I asked him when I was going to kick a ball, but he kept saying he had a practice match lined up for me soon – although he wouldn't actually commit to a date.

The most annoying thing about that day was that I had to pay £50 to train on the track. In other words, we'd driven a 200-mile round trip, paid £50 to run round a track a few times, and for what? I'd told Mel I was fit, he could see I was fit, so what was the point of that session? We left the training facility with no idea what was going to happen next – Mel didn't actually give me any clue about what plans he had other than a "practice match is in the pipeline." As the days went on, nothing actually materialised and I didn't get to play in the supposed practice match. Not surprisingly, I didn't hear back from Mel. It was a waste of a day – and £50.

With opportunities a bit thin on the ground, I went to several clubs including Mansfield Town for a few weeks at a time to do some training, just to keep fit more than anything. The manager at Mansfield was impressed with the way I trained and wanted to sign me, but he couldn't confirm how much he was going to pay me (which probably wouldn't have been much anyway). Nothing ever came of it and I was left to find somewhere else to train.

In the meantime, I tried to contact Mel Eves several times but he didn't return my calls. Then, a few weeks later, I was in Nottingham visiting my family and heard that a fellow Gambian, Njogu Demba-Nyrén was about to sign for Notts County. Njogu was meeting up with his agent in a local hotel and asked me to come along; I couldn't believe my eyes when he introduced me to his agent – it was Mel Eves. I looked straight at him and he asked how I was and we shook hands.

To show my disappointment I shook my head several times, suggesting he had been wrong not to get back to me, and then he started giving me all sorts of excuses. I stopped listening and told Njogu about my experience with Mel and then just walked away. In hindsight, maybe Mel was one of those agents who was waiting for the 'next big thing' to come along, and, to be fair, if I'd been 10 years younger, maybe that would have been me?

Chapter 7

What if...

"I want to be on that TV, doing what they're doing"

I'd been out of the game for nearly three years and had been training at several different clubs and having a few trials here and there to keep myself in shape. I didn't have an agent, as Harry wasn't active, so I had nobody there for me. It was hard to get myself motivated for anything and I was beginning to think my days in football were numbered.

It was during this time that I had a trial with Southport. However, it didn't turn out to be an entirely good experience because I pulled my hamstring on the first day.

I had to rest up for a few weeks and, in that time, I had physio sessions three hours a day, five days a week until I could start training again and, after about three weeks, my hamstring healed. The Southport manager Martin Foyle called and said he wanted me to come in and do a fitness test and, if I passed, I would be offered a contract. On that first day back, I did the training session in the morning and then got ready for the test in the afternoon. I was all geared up for the fitness test, which included a full medical and the usual running on a treadmill.

The following day, we trained again in the morning and in the afternoon played five-a-side on the Astro-Turf pitch. I'd started to get my mojo back and I was even doing some good stuff on the ball. However, during the game I held the ball under my foot, nobody was anywhere near me and I tried to take the ball and beat the nearest player to me. I stepped over the ball and felt (and heard) my ankle go. I dropped to the ground in so much pain that I screamed out loud.

Within a matter of seconds, the whole team surrounded me. The next thing I knew I was in an ambulance on the way to the nearest hospital – I was in agony and crying my eyes out. The strange thing about it is that I wasn't crying because of the pain, which was terrible, but because I knew 'this was it' – I knew it was a career-threatening injury. I called Fes to tell him the news and he assured me I'd be back in three months and I shouldn't worry. I'm not the type of person to give up easily, so I took Fes's words of encouragement on board and it made me feel a bit better. I'd waited for three years to get anywhere near a contract, so I thought three more months surely wouldn't hurt.

After that initial shock of breaking my ankle at such a crucial time in my career, I felt pretty upbeat and Fes kept telling me there was "one more deal to go" – certainly he wasn't about to give up on me, so I couldn't give up on myself either, could I?

It gets harder to recover, the older you get. I was 29 and I'd stayed out of the game for too long, so perhaps that was the contributing factor in why I'd broken my ankle – I just wasn't fit enough. Yes, I was fit but not match fit, certainly not fit enough to play 90 minutes. I probably became injury prone due to not training for long periods, which was ironic because I hardly got injured at the peak of my career. Everyone else, my family and Fes were remaining very positive, but in my own head and in my own heart I knew I wouldn't recover. I just didn't want to let those people around me know it; I was the only one who really knew how I felt.

When the specialists finally scanned my ankle and plastered it, the news arrived that I'd be out for five to six months. It was

August, so there was no chance I'd be kicking a ball until the New Year at least. Martin Foyle told me to be patient because he wanted me to come back to sign a contract, but I knew it would be a tough ask for me to wait that long.

After a few days in hospital, I decided to go back home to London and that train journey from Liverpool Lime Street was the longest three hours of my life. In one respect it was the worst journey of my life because I sat on that train, on my own, thinking about everything that had happened in my football career. All those good and bad memories came flooding back; to the first day I started playing football back in Gambia; to Watford; to Peckham; to England; to Millwall; to Spain and all the stops along the way. It made me so sad because I knew it had been such a rollercoaster journey, but now it was coming to an end. There was no turning back. I said to myself, "I can't do it anymore." My body was shattered and my mind more so. I was at a low ebb and I felt sorry for myself. I knew there was nothing else that could push me to start all over again. I had nothing left to give.

In another respect, that train ride had a big positive influence on my life in terms of what would be next for Cherno Samba. I'd decided that all of those memories I'd recalled would determine the direction I'd take for the rest of my life. I thought to myself, "I didn't do too badly." I'd achieved what I wanted to achieve in my life – to become a professional footballer and to put on that England jersey – those were my goals when I fell in love with football all those years ago. Those were my dreams from an early age, right from the moment I first watched a football match on TV, a Victory Shield game involving England Schoolboys and I told my Mum, "I want to be on that TV, doing what they're doing." That memory has stuck with me and it came back into my head when I was thinking through my life on that train. Based on my dreams at that tender age, I didn't do too badly – not many people can say they have achieved their goals in life and made dreams come true.

Having said that, there was a tinge of sadness and, dare I say, some bitterness thrown in there too, about what had gone wrong in my life and what I could have done better.

I began to question myself and wrote down some things along the lines of: what could have been if certain people hadn't stood in my way; if I'd have had a bit more support; if I'd have worked a little bit harder; if I'd have stood up and admitted, "It was partly my fault" and so on. I began to think, "if only…" then I may have got further in my career, to a better level than I actually did. As the train approached London, I looked at that piece of paper and tears flowed down my cheeks. I knew I couldn't rewind the past, but the past had developed me as a person and I was grateful for that.

I got off the train at Euston, gathered my thoughts, pulled myself back together again and told myself I'd start to make a plan for my future; however, the first thing I wanted to do was to see my wife and daughter and to block football out of my mind. For a whole month after returning home, I refused to watch any football on TV and I didn't even want to talk about football with my mates – I didn't want anything to do with it, full stop! I needed a break, but I had to return to the hospital for treatment on my ankle every two weeks, which put a stop to me going anywhere far for a while, certainly until they took the plaster off my leg.

After about six weeks, I decided to go to Gambia just to clear my head after the disappointment of losing out on a contract with Southport. I thought I'd be better off there because I'd be in the sun and by the sea so I could do some light workouts on the sand when I felt strong enough to do so. I didn't want to talk to anyone so, rightly or wrongly, I decided to lock myself away from the world – I thought that was the best thing for me to do at that particular time.

Growing up I had Fes as my best mate and as an older head he would sometimes question my decisions, but he wasn't in football so I tended, wrongly, not to listen to him. Sometimes I didn't have the mental strength I needed with the people around me. I truly believe you get what you deserve in this life. If you try and skip certain situations or if you try and run before you can walk that's when you can fall down – and I fell down a lot. I know a lot of young lads who skipped education and went straight to crime – that was their choice, and that's fine, but they paid the consequences for that decision. Conversely, if you have leadership in your life and have people around you who care about you, then you grow up a better person and you'll be in a position to make better decisions.

Now here's the thing, and I'll go into this later on, but for the young people reading this book, I have a simple message – there are no short cuts in life – none! I know that's not a hard and fast rule, but if you find a short cut, believe me, you will pay the consequences somehow. As with everything, there are exceptions to the rule, but they are few and far between and that's where the balance is all screwed up. In football, the exceptions to the rule are put in front of a magnifying glass for all to see.

I came back to London after four months in Gambia with an opportunity waiting for me to play for a non-league team called Chasetown, which is in Staffordshire. Their manager was Marcus Law, and Ian Seddon, my new agent by this time, arranged for me to meet him with a view to me being a player/coach. At the back of my mind, I knew my leg wasn't 100%, but I went to meet up with Marcus all the same. I started off helping with the coaching sessions but soon afterwards Marcus left the club because he was offered the vacant Kettering job. The Chasetown chairman Mike Joiner asked me to stay with the club to help on the coaching staff when the new manager arrived.

It was my first pre-season in a long while and I trained for several weeks until our first friendly game. It was a usual pre-season schedule where the manager chopped and changed the team. I played the last ten minutes of the first game but when the final whistle blew, I knew that my time was up – I was knackered and it broke me in two.

I remember walking to the changing room after the game and all sorts of negative thoughts flooded my head – it was only natural that I felt that way. My head was banging but deep down I knew I wouldn't play again. The first thing I did that night was to speak to Ian and break the news to him, "Ian, I think this is it." Ian tried to calm me down and advised me to sleep on it and told me he'd call me in the morning. I think he was in shock as well and didn't want to speak about anything else after that. As soon as I'd put the phone down to him, I cried my eyes out. It was only then I started to think, "What am I going to do?" I didn't sleep that night and I didn't eat, which was pretty unheard of for me, but again, it was a natural reaction to bad news. All night, I couldn't stop thinking about my future until a time when I just couldn't think any more.

The next day, Ian kept his promise, and called me and asked me a direct question, "What do you think?" My answer hadn't changed, "Yeah, I've got to be honest with myself here, I'm really emotional right now but this is it. I've just played 10 minutes of a pre-season friendly and I can't run. I just can't do the things I used to do. I can still feel my leg – I can't do it." While I was talking to Ian, tears were flooding down my cheeks once more and I remember the tone of his voice was down as well – I think he also knew it was over. He wanted to gauge my reaction and make sure I was making the right decision – and in his mind I had done just that. I think he was relieved in a way and immediately he said I should post something on my Twitter and Facebook accounts about my retirement from the game.

This is what I drafted for my Twitter account:

> It is with sadness that I officially announce my retirement from football in order to focus on moving on to the next chapter of my career, which is to attain my coaching badges.

I want to thank my family, friends and the special fans for being with me on this great journey. Their love and support has been my rock and I could not have done better without their support.

Many other people played a huge part in my career from when I started as a child, but I want to say a big Thank You in particular to Richard Bate, Harry Gerber and Ian Seddon for their tremendous support during the course of my career. Thank you for the coaching and mentoring!

Ever since I was a kid, all I dreamed of was to become a professional football player and to play for England. Representing England until U21 level and the Scorpions of The Gambia has been a great joy for my family and me. Both nations played a part in helping that dream come true for me and for that, I can just say THANK YOU!

The past few years have been difficult for me, as I couldn't get back on the pitch due to persistent ankle injuries and that is the main reason I have decided to finally call it a day.

It has been an honour for me to grace the field with great players, playing with and against them. I am thankful for the managers, clubs and countries that I have passed through in my career as well as my teammates, it has been an honour working with you and sharing the field playing the game we all love.

My sincere thanks to Millwall and everyone associated with the football club, for they gave me the chance to begin my career with them.

The media have also contributed a lot in my career, as I might not be where I am today without their exposure and writing about me. My sincere gratitude to them as I consider them partners in football development.

My greatest appreciation to the fans for being with me on this journey from day one. I cannot thank you enough. Finally, it is with sadness and joy that I bring an end to this fantastic FIFTEEN-YEAR career of mine, I am grateful for all the opportunities that the sport brought me.

THANK YOU!!!

It took me nearly two days to post the statement but when I actually pressed the send button it was like a big weight had been taken off my shoulders – it was such a relief to make the biggest decision of my whole life and there was no turning back. I don't know why I was so scared of posting the statement. Maybe I was scared of the reaction it may have caused, plus I was probably scared to speak to people about it. As soon as I'd posted that statement, I prayed to God for a full 45 minutes, crying but also thinking I'd just done the right thing. I knew it was a positive thing and the best thing for me but I also had faith in God that he'd made the best decision for me too.

Within a few minutes of my posts going viral, I started receiving Tweets back – my Twitter account went crazy, my phone went crazy and messages flooded my phone. I had radio stations ring me up asking for me to talk to them and Ian also received calls asking for me to make some comment.

From that day on, I have never looked back, but at the time I didn't think I'd ever be able to do that.

It seemed that my playing days had ended almost as quickly as they'd begun, and I was now looking forward to the next chapter of my life.

Chapter 8

England, Wayne Rooney and My Football Father

*"Number one – be a decent human being,
Number two – be a decent footballer"*

Dick Bate
Former England Youth Team Head Coach

Playing for England was my best time as a professional footballer – I loved every minute of it. It was more like playing for a club than playing for your national team. Even though my club career was a bit hit-and-miss at times, I will always be grateful to the England set-up for keeping their faith in me and especially to my coach and good friend, the late Dick Bate. I will always hold him in such high regard because he helped and advised me throughout my England career at all levels right up until he passed away.

He was just a great man – one of the greatest men I have ever known in my life, in fact.

Even during periods where I had fallen out of favour at my clubs, Dick was there to advise me, not just on football matters but on personal issues as well. I call him my 'football father' because he effectively groomed me into the England system from an early age. I will be eternally grateful to Dick for sharing his wealth of knowledge with me. Words aren't enough for the love and respect I have for him.

Dick always had confidence in me, and my ability, even during periods when I had no confidence in myself. From the first time I met him, he left his mark on me and the other England players, because he made himself available to us, all the time. I think that helped us, especially when we started playing for England at a young age. Every time I've felt the need to call him, I have always done so without hesitation, whether it was to listen to his words of wisdom or seek his advice on what my next move should be. He has always been there for me; even when he's miles away he has time to speak to me.

I was 13 or 14 years old and playing for Millwall Under-15s when I was made aware I was being watched by the England scouts. I will never forget the day I was picked for my first trials session. There were about 50 of us who were selected for a trial at Lilleshall – players from all different clubs from all over the country. From those 50 hopefuls, I think only David Bentley and I stood out – because we didn't actually play in the trials. I said to David, "Everyone else's playing – there's only me and you standing here". He nudged me and replied, "Listen, they know what we can do. Don't worry about it – they've already picked us". What David said during that trial was spot-on – we were a cut-above the rest and we were the first two players to get selected because Dick already knew what we could do.

I will never forget the first time I met Dick. I think it was Joel Kitamirike (a young defender at Chelsea) who was marking me during another England trial and the first words I heard Dick shout were, "What a tussle." We were both big lads and after the session I heard him talking about the tussle between us on the pitch and I remember him saying, "...but I think Cherno came out on top". As a young player, I needed someone like him around me, to guide me and coax me and Dick was that guy from day one. Years later, Dick told me he liked my movement off the ball in my first game, even though I didn't touch the ball for the first 20 minutes and that's what made him select me. He felt that made me an intelligent player who knew the basics and how to bring others into the game at such a young age. I knew I had all the attributes to be a professional footballer – I had all the moves, the touches and I had a football brain, but to be told I was good enough to play for England from such a young age was unreal. Dick told me I moved like an adult, on and off the ball and I scored goals when I wanted to. I was lethal and I felt that I had it all. I was so confident with the ball, I was bordering on arrogance when I was younger.

The one thing I wanted to do after I got selected for my first actual squad was a bit unusual. I phoned Harry first and said I wanted to write to Dick via the FA to tell him how I felt about playing football and what playing for England would mean to me. Harry thought it was a great idea and encouraged me to do it. I don't know why I did it if I'm honest. It wasn't meant to be a grovelling letter, but I wanted to thank him for the opportunity and assured him I would never let him down, so I guess I wanted to get noticed. I would imagine not many prospective footballers have gone to such lengths, but I wanted to do something a bit different.

I was constantly thinking about football when I was at St Joseph's Academy and, if I recall, I was in an arts and crafts class when I wrote a long letter to Dick (while I was supposed to be drawing, painting or something). The letter started along the lines:

Dear Dick,

I, Cherno Samba, am writing you this letter. I hope you are well and in good health? Thank you for selecting me for my first England cap. I want you to know that I would do all I can to not let you down and always do my best for the team...

The letter went on and obviously got to Dick and it must have done the trick because I got picked for a Victory Shield match against Northern Ireland on 15th October 1999, shortly after sending it.

I must admit, the letter to the FA was only half of the story. At that time, I didn't have a British passport; I'd applied for my passport a few months beforehand, but it had been held up and it wouldn't have been ready in time for me to play in the Victory Shield game. Just because I had been picked for the England squad didn't guarantee me anything.

So, when I eventually made the England squad, Dick told all the successful players to bring their passports with them when we next met up. Knowing my passport was at the Passport Office and hadn't been processed yet, I didn't say anything, which was probably the wrong thing to do but I was worried about what would have happened if I owned up. I was thinking I'd be in trouble and get dropped from the squad, so I was reluctant to say anything that would have jeopardised my England future. I was hoping that I would receive my passport before our next meeting – anybody else would have done the same, I'm sure.

When the day came to present our passports, I still hadn't received mine and I was so scared before I went in to see Dick. I was scared that he might say I was ineligible to play for England. There were 18 of us who had been selected for the first time and everyone except for me had a British passport. I was terrified when my name was called out and when I went in to see Dick I was shaking like a leaf. I felt like I just wanted to go home and when I told him about my passport application, he stood there for what must have been several minutes until he said, "There is no time to write to the Passport Office so tomorrow morning, you'll go with one of our staff to the Liverpool Passport Office and we'll see what the hold up is, and if there is anything we can do to help". From that moment on, I knew I would love and respect Dick Bate. I walked out of that room with tears rolling down my face, tears of happiness and relief. I couldn't believe it – it was like a dream come true. Maybe you'd call it fate – it was definitely meant to be. As soon as I got out of that room I called Harry and told him the news.

The next day, Harry, one of the FA staff and myself went to the Passport Office in Liverpool, where we were able to talk to someone personally about my application. We were informed that, although my passport had been approved, it was still "in the system" and it could take another month or so for me to receive my passport. After explaining the 'emergency', we requested that the process be fast-tracked, and we were then informed that I would receive my passport in time to play in the game.

That was a beautiful day – no doubt about it – if it wasn't for Dick's intervention and advice it would have taken a lot longer and I would have missed my England debut.

When it came to my debut against Northern Ireland in that Victory Shield tie, I stood in line to sing the National Anthem and glanced over to Dick standing in the dugout and a few tears rolled down my face, but I stuck out my chest and sang my heart out. I was as proud as anyone that day. I wanted to make an impression and in my heart I wanted to do well for Dick more than anyone else. That was the respect I had for the man.

As I've mentioned before, the FA notified us by letter when we were called up into an England squad a few weeks before an international game. I used to get excited when the letter dropped on the doorstep but on one occasion I was on holiday in Gambia when Mum and Alhajie notified me that I'd received a call-up letter for a mini-tournament in Portugal. Harry told me I needed to train before the game so he asked the Gambian national coach if I could train with them to pick up my fitness before the international match and he was only too happy to allow me to train for a couple of weeks. So, instead of travelling from England with the rest of the squad the FA booked me on a flight from Gambia to Portugal.

That tournament in Portugal was special for me because it was the first time I met Dick's wife, Maggie and it was such an honour for me because it cemented our growing friendship. We had just landed back in London and before we all went our separate ways, Dick stopped me and pointed over to a lady waiting for him, "See that lady over there? Go and see her. She has a lot to do with my success – go and say 'Hello'." I did as I was told and said, "Hi, my name is Cherno." Maggie obviously knew who I was because she replied, "Ah, Cherno, how lovely to meet you. I'm Maggie, Dick's wife. I've heard all about you. Well done," and she gave me a hug and a kiss. For me, moments like that are precious and that I will cherish for the rest of my life. I said to myself, "That's my England manager introducing me to his wife. Wow!" I was so happy and joyful after that moment that I went back to speak to Dick with a smile as wide as the ocean and he said, "Well done lad." Those are the moments you can't relive.

****

In November 2011 Maggie asked me to write another letter, this time to explain how Dick had helped me progress in my England career since I'd first written to him back in my school days. The letter touched me so much I was actually crying as I wrote it. This is the letter I wrote to the FA in support of Dick:

Dear Mr Rutter,

RE – SUPPORT LETTER FOR RICHARD BATE

In life you meet certain people that change your life for good and Richard Bate changed mine for the best.

I met Richard at the age of 14 when he identified me at an England trial. He coached me from Under 15 through to Under 19. During this period till today, I see Richard as a father to me. I will proudly say that Richard brought out the best in me not only on the pitch, but in life as a whole. He instilled decency in me and gave me a better outlook on life.

Anybody that meets Richard cannot help but love him, as he is the most honest, caring, and respectful, honourable and supportive man. Believe me when I say there aren't enough words to describe Richard Bate. Moments when I lost hope and thought I was at the end of my career, Richard always was my guardian angel. He lifts me back on my feet and puts me back on the right track. And can you believe, he recently just saved me when I lost all hope.

Tell me, can you help not always honouring a man such as Richard. I personally cannot help it hence why I always stayed in touch with him no matter what side of the world I am on. I would go on and on about Richard but because words are not enough to say what I want to say and my emotions are getting the best of me talking about him.

I would like to conclude by saying to each and every person who happens to read this that I, Cherno Samba, am very honoured to have had the privilege to not only work with Richard but to meet him.

Therefore, I cannot see any other man out there that deserves this award more than Richard Bate. I will happily say that I have not looked back since meeting him.

Yours truly,

CHERNO SAMBA

The idea of sending a letter to the FA was to recommend Dick for an award of some kind for all the years he's spent in the game and I'd like to think I helped his cause because, in

December 2013, Dick was awarded The Lifetime Contribution Award from the FA. To put his achievement into perspective, Dick has helped so many of the country's top coaches in the last 20 years to pass their qualifications.

So, as you can see I think most highly of Dick Bate. He is a person who, when he speaks, you listen. Not only that you need to be on your best behaviour at all times, and you need to be on your guard, too. I put Dick in the 'old school headmaster' category, which is a compliment by the way because he commands and demands respect.

Dick had a very structured approach to training and he was very disciplined, which isn't a bad thing. He's the type of coach who actually joined in with the training and he would demonstrate a certain move by doing it himself. Even though I said he's 'old school' he was very much a progressive coach and has evolved with the game over the years while keeping the same philosophy; that reflects how clever and knowledgeable he is. Some coaches are either defensive or offensive-minded, but Dick believed in both ways of playing, which was great for me. Not only did he teach you how to defend, but he also let you play your natural game, which in my case was always trying to get forward. Ironically, his favoured formation was having three forwards in a 4-3-3, which, I must admit I hated (sorry Dick) because I played best with someone up front alongside me. I also loved being the lone striker but I never complained because all I wanted to do was to play football, whatever the position. Dick would sometimes change the formation depending on how the game was going and would partner me with another striker from time-to-time.

I was making runs for the ball, I was very raw and all I wanted to do was turn, run with the ball then shoot, but Dick taught me how to hold the ball up. He also instilled the discipline in me that is required to be a modern footballer. In life, Dick also instilled humanity in me by talking to me in terms of life experiences and trying to make me a decent human being. His philosophy was simple:

Number one, be a decent human being.
Number two, be a decent footballer.

To me, that was a priceless piece of advice and I bet most coaches in the game wouldn't teach you things like that – but I surely will when I become a coach.

England hosted the European Under-16 finals in 2001 and I played in every game until the semi-finals, when we lost to France, who went on to play Spain in the final. I scored in the quarter final against Germany and we actually beat them on penalties, would you believe? We all went to watch the final at the Stadium of Light in Sunderland, and for some reason a blonde-haired lad called Fernando Torres fascinated me. He subsequently became a world-class striker. I just thought he was a tall striker who could run, head the ball well and score goals. It's crazy to think that I watched Torres at that young age and only a few years later he became a household name. Incidentally, Torres was top scorer with seven goals in that tournament.

On the French side the only player that stuck out for me was Anthony Le Tallec, but there was a German lad called David Odonkor, who for me was the one. He was unbelievable for our age group and was the most talked-about player in Germany. I'll never forget what he said to me as we were walking along the corridor, waiting to go out onto the pitch, "You're very good player – very fast. I like you. We talked about you for 30 minutes, how to mark you". I also spoke to Andreas Spann and he told me the same, that the German coach had spent 30 minutes talking about how to mark me. It was such a big compliment that the Germans thought I was their main threat and they'd spent that time talking about me, the "danger man number 9". In fact, Spann even asked me to come and play in Germany – that was really humbling for me.

Maybe I should have taken his advice.

Until I reached the age of 16, I played in teams a year above my own age group, which was no big deal for me as I'd been doing it all my life. Prior to the 2002 Under-17 European Championships we went on a three-week trip to Brazil. Well, words can't describe that trip – it was such an amazing few weeks. We played against the likes of Brazil, South Korea, Mexico and France but we didn't win any of the games. Brazil had an exceptional side and a tall striker called Leandro stuck out. I thought he would have been a star but I don't think he made it. He was unbelievable during the game against us though. The main problems for us were the conditions; it was hot (above 40C) and we weren't used to the humidity – we were fatigued. I think we lost 5-0 to the host nation – they battered us. Having said that, it was an experience of a lifetime just to go out there and play against the Brazilians. I will never forget that amazing place.

We had some great coaches in the England set-up including Dick, Clive Allen, Nigel Pearson and Kenny Swain. I worked closely with Clive because he was our striker coach and he taught me how to finish properly – he was a great finisher himself in his day and you saw that when he coached us. He told me finishing can become a habit and he was right. Clive was an infectious character; he was so motivated and his adrenalin was unbelievable. He was energetic, so energetic – he always made me feel very confident in my own ability. Just like Dick Bate, when he spoke you just had to listen. He'd sit us down and talk to us all the time; talk to us about what we were doing right, what we had to work on and what we were doing wrong. Very often he'd be there standing in front of us and he'd suddenly throw the ball in a random direction and quickly say something like, "Right Cherno, where would you put it?" and we'd sit down again and carry on listening to him. Clive is a top bloke and I learned so much from him for the three or four years he was coaching us.

While we were in Brazil, I remember I wasn't feeling great and my training was sloppy that day. I don't know what was up with me and I had no answer other than that I had fierce competition for my place as Darren Bent had been called up and I was warned he was after my starting place. Dick knew I was feeling low, so he called me into his office following a training session, told me my training wasn't good enough and asked me why. He asked me if the reason had anything to do with Darren's call up. Darren and I had a big rivalry because we were vying for the same position and we were both talented players, but for me it was nothing more than a friendly rivalry. Benty was being played out wide, he was knocking on the door for a starting place in the Ipswich Town first team and was desperate to start for the England Under-17s. I was already aware of his goal-scoring records for his club and now we were competing for the same England starting place.

I told Dick that I was scared but my sloppy training had nothing to do with Darren's inclusion to the squad. He quickly reassured me by saying, "You don't have to be scared. Go out there and show me what you can do. You are my number one striker. Don't you ever forget that". You know, that chat with Dick was like a weight had been lifted off my shoulders. I went back onto the training ground and felt my normal relaxed and calm self and started training harder than I had done for a few days. Sometimes, players just need an arm around them and some words of encouragement to get them back in the right frame of mind – I know I did from time-to-time when my confidence was low.

Among the players in my age group there was one special talent that stood out above everyone else and his name was Wayne Rooney. I had been the first name on the team sheet for various England squads with Wayne acting as my understudy. Yes, I was always keeping Wayne on the bench at one stage. We got on really well from day one and I remember the first time we met was when we both got called up for the Under 17s. We'd all been given official England suits and ties to wear but Wayne being Wayne, he turned up to the training camp wearing a white Lacoste tracksuit and headphones, listening to his favourite hip-hop music. He had just been signed by Everton at the time and had hit the headlines, but he hadn't made his England debut yet. I asked him why he wasn't wearing his shirt and tie and he replied, "I don't like it – I prefer wearing a tracksuit". That was the moment I knew this kid had something about him and was destined for stardom.

Wayne was always the best trainer in our group and in fact was probably the best trainer I've ever known. He always kept himself in good shape and trained hard, making sure he improved in every session. We were preparing for an Under-17s game against Slovakia and Wayne was pencilled in for a place on the bench, though he was a bit confused as to why he was only on the bench. Everyone could see he'd performed well in training, but Dick had a dilemma whether to start him or bench him and he chose the latter. However, during the day Dick had no alternative but to change his starting line-up and, instead of using me as a lone striker, he went with two up-front, pairing me with Wayne so he could finally make his debut.

Wayne was a fighter, always aggressive in training – not in a bad way but more competitive than anything else. He was a strong lad from a very early age and I remember he got me in a headlock during a play fight and I couldn't get out of it due to his strength. I was a big strong lad as well, but Wayne was so powerful – I hadn't realised just how powerful he was.

I always knew he would make it big time because of his skill and aggression; there was something special about him, even at the age of 15. He's matured and he's done well in his career, so fair play to him. Wayne's deserved all of his scoring records and the captain's armband too.

With young players from so many different clubs in the England setup, the talk was almost always about our respective clubs and what was happening there – that's all we seemed to talk about really, that and the game we'd just played in. All I wanted to do was to play at the highest level and I had hoped Liverpool would give me that opportunity. In fact, one of the reasons why I nearly signed for Liverpool was because I had spoken to John Welsh, who was our vice-captain and had just broken into their first team squad around that time. John was a great friend to me and I think he tried to persuade the club to sign me. In my experience, it often happens that players get called up for their country and will talk up their own clubs in the hope of making moves happen.

When we played for the younger England teams under the age of 21, we didn't get paid as such; we received expenses in terms of a mileage allowance to and from home to the game, which to a 15 or 16-year old was still a lot of money. I'd have played for nothing anyway because it was a privilege to wear the shirt. The England lads were like family to me and every time I read the letter informing me I'd been selected for the squad it sent shivers down my spine. Once I knew I was in the squad, I'd start to look down the list of names of people who had been selected to make sure my mates had been called up. After that, I just couldn't wait to join up with the rest of the lads – it could be up to three weeks away, so that time tended to drag on.

Looking back at my time with England, I recall the professionalism of the set-up from the minute we walked into the training camp to the minute we left to go back to our clubs. It couldn't have been more well organised because we were looked after as soon as we checked in; we were nourished, watered and we had an abundance of staff looking after our needs every single day. In a nutshell, we were actually spoilt, which was great at the time and we felt special.

However, now that I'm no longer part of that set-up, I look back and I question whether it was such a good thing to be so spoilt. You name it, we had it; massages, saunas or steams whenever we wanted; we had food provided to suit everyone's dietary needs – at any time of the day we wanted. The majority of the players involved in the England squads were already earning large sums of money from their clubs and that in itself was another issue. I can't be sure, but I can guess the other top European countries didn't pamper their young players like we did and probably still do.

Being spoilt extended further than being fed, watered and pampered with massages and saunas. The pitches we trained on were first-class and the hotels we stayed in were five-star. I can sit here now and give my opinion because I've been through it all and if there were one thing I could change, that would be it. In fact, hypothetically, if I ever took charge of the FA I'd certainly tone down all of the pampering that the young England lads enjoy because I don't think it's at all necessary. I can understand why the FA has to do it – England is one of the leading football nations in the world and I suppose it's kind of expected of them. Playing for your club was more or less the same and I can guarantee now that today's players are super-spoilt, even more so that we were with England. There's so much money in the game now; it's become an entertainment industry and everything is so much more glamorous – or so it seems.

When I recall playing against countries that were less fortunate than England, those countries who didn't have what we had, I really believe it made them even hungrier to win – maybe they wanted it more? That doesn't mean we didn't want it, but they had more to prove. In short, those so-called 'lesser' nations wanted to be where we were.

****

Only in England do you struggle to find another club after getting released from a club, even though you have played at all levels of the national team. If you play for any other national team at Under-21 level, you'll still be in the game at a top-level club for a long time. The reason for that block-age is because we have so many foreign players playing at the top level that our quality youngsters rarely get a look in, especially at the top clubs in the Premier League. They get as far as the Under-21s but don't progress and find them-selves in the lower leagues.

Young English players hardly ever go abroad to play, but I was the exception to the rule. I was also one of very few England Under-21 players ever to play abroad. I just wanted to play at a high level and I had my chance. At the time I got called up to play against Russia in February 2005, I was at a low ebb because I wasn't getting a fair chance at my club side and I was feeling personally rejected. I contacted Dick Bate and asked him who else had been called up and he reeled of the list with the likes of Wayne Routledge, Danny Graham, Gary Cahill, Simon Francis, Bradley Wright-Phillips and Richard Chaplow. We had a strong squad and some of those names were playing first-team football, week in, week out, unlike me who was warming the bench at Cádiz.

Although I was pleased to be selected, I had a feeling inside me that I would start on the bench or not be picked at all. However, to my surprise, John Peacock called me the night before the game and told me I was doing really well in training and asked me how I was feeling. I told him I was feeling good; I felt great in training and was back to something like my old self, doing some tricks, which caught the coaches' eyes. John obviously knew I was feeling good so I didn't really need to tell him. I must have impressed the coaches to a certain extent because they made a few jokes about my skills, "We're not playing in Spain now, Cherno..."

The game came and went. John played 4-3-3 and I played out on the right in the number 7 shirt and had a good game. I jus-tified my selection, taking players on and tracking back when required, but most of all I enjoyed it. Even though I didn't score, I had a great chance in the second half but missed it – after the game, Bradley's dad, Ian Wright told me off. He explained to me what I should have done in that situation. Who was I to argue with the Arsenal legend?

Thoughts of playing for Cádiz were a million miles away – it was a total contrast and that was how I wanted to feel playing football every week, win, lose or draw. I just wanted to get that buzz back from playing the game I loved. I really enjoyed that day.

****

As you are aware by now, I loved every minute of playing for England. It's something I'm very proud of and now I'm retired I'm still a big fan and watch all their games on TV. Every England supporter knows we have not performed well enough at tournaments, for whatever reason. Whoever the England manager is at the time, they are unable to unlock the potential we always show by getting through the group stages. Everybody has his or her own views on what is wrong with the whole England setup; I have my own view too and it's a view from the inside as I've seen it at close quarters.

I'm obviously talking about my own experiences here, but one of the problems we have is that young England players have developed a belief that most foreign teams are better than us. When we are at youth team level, we talk about other teams among ourselves and it becomes a belief that teams like Germany, Spain, Italy and Brazil are better than us. Conversations along the lines of, "Did you see that Brazilian striker last night – he was awesome..." go on in the dressing room all the time. The young players always seem to be in awe of their counterparts – the players they are up against on the pitch.

Here's an example. We played Italy at youth level and I was explaining to one of my England teammates where he should be passing the ball to me for me to pick it up and I will always remember his response, "Fuck off Chern. As if the ball's going to get to you mate. Come on we're playing against Italy. You've got no chance." At the time we laughed about it, but looking back those comments said something about the reality of why England sometimes play with fear.

Can you imagine a 15 or 16-year old young England team player going into a game against Italy, Spain or Germany believing they are inferior to the opposition? These lads will grow up with that lack of belief and when they eventually get into the Under-21s and the first team, that negativity will surely be ingrained in them.

I really believe there is a fear factor associated with the England team and it affects their performances – the Iceland match was a prime example of that theory in action. There is a mentality issue with the players. Compare that attitude with all those new African nations like Ghana who have the belief they can do it, even though they may not have the best players to choose from. Another example would be Ireland in World Cup '94, who beat Italy through sheer determination and belief.

Personally, I don't think some of us English footballers are as mentally strong as our foreign counterparts. The England football team seem to have lost that winning mentality, not in the last few years but I think over the last twenty years or more. We had the players to win that game against Iceland but we turned up and didn't know what to do with the ball on the day. We big up all these guys in the Premier League, week in, week out but when they put on an England shirt they seem to turn to jelly. We need someone to get into the players' heads. Who that person is, I just don't know.

England have had some well-respected managers over recent years in the likes of Capello, but he couldn't get a winning side together in a major tournament, even with the talent we had at the time. That leads me to think that it's the players who are the real failures. You could get Pep Guardiola to manage England and in my opinion we would still fail – I really believe that. If you look at the Spanish national side some 15 years ago, they were major under-achievers before Luis Aragonés and then Vincente del Bosque came along and shook the whole thing up and made them into a winning machine. It can be done!

Another problem we have in this country is the media, who don't help our national team because they think we are still a super-power nation who should be winning every competition we enter. Now, that's a bigger issue and it's been going on ever since 1966.

However, I believe the FA is currently introducing a new directive on youth football in England. In my opinion, the number one issue concerns the structure of our youth system, which is out-dated in my book. If you go to the top nations of football, like Germany, Spain, Brazil, Argentina, France or wherever you'll find from youth level up to Under-17 they never play 11-a-side – they play anything between 5-a-side to 8-a-side and on a reduced sized pitch – and have been doing so for years. While in England, we only recently started training our youth players from an early age to play games on reduced-sized pitches and not full 11-a-side pitches.

Although we are on the right course as a nation to improve our football, I think we are still a long way behind.

The thing about playing on a smaller pitch in an 8-a-side game is that it teaches you about keeping possession. It's more comfortable for players to control the ball on smaller pitches because players know how to manoeuvre, run and pass the ball in tight spaces. It's fairly simple stuff when you think about it, but we don't seem to have learned from the top countries yet.

In my view, it's important that England have a playing identity – Spain have a quick-tempo pass and move game and the Italians have a rigid defensive system, with a quick counter-attack. At the moment, I don't think we have a 'style', although I realise a system can change from game-to-game.

As for a lack of English managers – well that's another story.

Chapter 9

Playing for Gambia

"Go for it son. I think the time is right for you"

Dick Bate
Former England Youth Team Head Coach

At the age of 22, I was without a club, too old to continue playing for England at Under-21 level and there was little chance I'd be considered to fulfil my ultimate ambition of playing for the senior squad unless I was playing in a top league. I'd played at all levels of the England youth system but now I'd hit the buffers.

For many years I'd heard that my 'home' country Gambia had been chasing me to play for the national side, so I started to think seriously about the opportunity to play for them at full international level. Their head coach was a Belgian called Paul Put who had a low-key football career to say the least. In fact, I don't think he played at any sort of level. Anyway, I'd always wanted to prove myself as a full international and Paul contacted Harry during the summer of 2008 to see if I was available to play for my country of birth. Harry then phoned me to see what I thought about the idea. I gave Harry the green light to arrange a meeting with Paul, who came all the way from Gambia to England to meet us. They even got the Chief of Security and the Gambian President to call me, trying to persuade me to play for the national side, "This is your country. You have an opportunity here".

At first I wasn't convinced and I felt hesitant. Why? Well, playing for any African nation is hard because the pressure the media puts on the players and the manager is ten-times worse than the pressure put on by the media when you play for England. Football becomes 'everything' to the majority of people and the level of publicity footballers of national sides get is insane. As an example, when Ghanaian captain Asamoah Gyan missed that penalty in the 2010 World Cup he had death threats back home – it was serious and there have been other examples in the past, too. Making the decision to play for my country of birth should have been be a no-brainer but it wasn't an easy decision to make – did I want the pressure of being threatened, or my family being threatened if it all turned sour?

I decided to put off making a decision until I had spoken to my 'football father', Dick Bate. Of course, he urged me to say "yes" and said, "Go for it son. I think the time is right for you to have to look at your limitations, so go for it." As soon as he said that, I was at ease and ready to commit to Gambia.

Once I'd decided, Harry called Paul Put to give him my answer but warned him that if I were made a scapegoat, I would be pulled out of the set-up immediately. He also said I wouldn't be talking to the Gambian media. Paul told Harry he wanted to build a team around me and I was his number one – I was going to be the main guy – and when I heard what he'd said, it convinced me even more and made me feel wanted. It was nice to hear those words. All I wanted to do was to keep my head down and play my normal game for my country. A short time later, I received a letter to tell me I'd been called up to play against Liberia at home in an African Cup of Nations qualifier on 6th September 2008.

I flew to Gambia full of optimism, full of hope and full of life. It was a new beginning for me. I was so happy and when I arrived in the country, my name was everywhere in the media and everyone was talking about me. It was like 'the prodigal son' had returned. Even though there was supposed to have been a media ban on me, the press swarmed on me as I arrived at Banjul airport, yet I managed to swerve them and they soon left me alone. I only had a day or so to settle in before I started to train with my new teammates and that was when I realised that Gambia were light years away from almost every other football nation. One or two days before the game, the lads would go out with their wives and girlfriends at night and I wasn't used to seeing that. The level of professionalism I was used to in England and Spain just wasn't there. When I told some of the players that sort of thing wasn't allowed in other countries, they couldn't believe it – it was normal for them to stay out late before a big game but I wanted to relax and get an early night.

At this point, I should mention an old friend of mine, Aziz Corr Nyang, who I met when we linked up with the Gambian national side. He and I grew up together in Gambia and played football as 5 or 6 year olds before I left for England. We'd obviously heard about each other's careers in the meantime but we hadn't seen each other since 1990. It was my first call-up and Aziz knew I'd been selected for the squad, so he came looking for me in the hotel and when he found me we embraced and hugged each other. It was one of those unbelievable moments I'll never forget, seeing an old friend after such a long time and with our careers having gone in different directions. It was great to link up with him again.

I soon came to realise that playing for Gambia would be a wholly different experience and nothing like playing for England, where everything is done for you. In Gambia, nothing is done for you – for example, you have to arrange and pay for your travel on the promise that the Gambian FA would reimburse you but, in reality, you'd never get anything back from them. Bonuses too – you'd never receive them. On my debut for Gambia, I remember the players were threatening to strike; they threatened not to play in the game against Liberia unless their bonuses were paid from the previous game. That was the time I began to see it would be a bizarre experience playing for Gambia. I had to intervene and remind the boys that we were playing for our country – I'd have played for free and so should they. I think they thought I was mad. However, they stuck to their guns, the Gambian FA paid up and we played the game, but the money wasn't fantastic, if I'm honest.

It was like I'd been transported back to another era. The infra-structure and professionalism in the game over there just wasn't what I'd been used to and one of the most striking dif-ferences was the pitches we had to train and play our games on. It seemed they hadn't improved very much in the 15 years since I'd left. Instead of moaning, I decided I had no choice to get used to the hard, worn out pitches. The main stadium where we played our home games and trained was called the Independence Stadium in Bakau – it was the only proper stadium in the country.

Match day approached and I was looking forward to playing a major part in the game – just as I'd been promised by the coach, but Paul Put named me as a substitute. I was on the bench for my first game! To say I wasn't happy is an under-statement. I hadn't come all that way to sit on the bench and I later found out what Paul's game was; he was basically trying to put down my so-called ego because I'd made the country wait for 15 years to accept an invitation to play for them, so he probably thought he'd make me wait for my debut. The Gambian FA had been chasing me for such a long time to play for them, but it appeared the coach didn't like me being so popular with the fans and wanted to teach me a lesson. He obviously thought I was getting more headlines than him and he wanted to take me down a peg or two, so he benched me. He had no idea what that was doing to my confidence.

The majority of the 30,000 fans had come to see what I could do – they were singing my name all through the 90 minutes and they went wild as I warmed up along the touchline. It was so loud that the hairs on the back of my neck stood up.

Ever since I'd arrived in the country, all they'd heard about was Cherno Samba and the reception I received changed everything. I wasn't happy at being stuck on the bench but the crowd had faith in me so I suddenly got renewed motivation to do something special if and when I got onto the pitch.

I was brought on in the second half with 15 minutes to go and within 10 seconds the ball came to me, I controlled it with the outside of my foot and the crowd went wild. It was a technique they hadn't seen before and once I'd controlled the ball I went on a run down the wing, passed a diagonal ball to Omar Koroma and he passed it back to me to fire a shot which was saved by the 'keeper. The crowd went wild again. Suddenly, I'd forgotten about the embarrassment I'd felt about being benched and got stuck into the game. We won 3-0 and I was so happy to have finally played for Gambia.

With the first game under my belt, I was called up for a game against Senegal in another African Cup of Nations qualifier. Again, I turned up on the day thinking that I'd made an impact on my debut, so surely I'd be picked in the starting line-up. Everyone who witnessed my debut saw what I could do – a starting place was surely guaranteed? Well, no! I was named on the bench again and I was even more miffed.

From then on, I started to wonder what I'd have to do to get a start. To be perfectly honest, the players I was playing with weren't at my level – none of them had my experience. "Come on show some respect, Paul," I thought to myself. When I heard the news, I immediately called Harry, who told me not to worry and to just get on with it, so I took his advice. Even my Gambian teammates couldn't believe I hadn't been picked to start, so I asked to speak to Paul before the next match. I assured him I wasn't trying to cause trouble, but I told him he was taking the piss. He responded in the usual way, by diverting the question and saying things like, "You're a skilful player and I like you but...." There was always a 'but'. They were just words that meant nothing to me. He was trying to calm things down, so I left it at that.

Three hours before the important qualifier with Senegal, we had a pre-match meal consisting of rice, which was so oily it was inedible. How could you eat a plate of oily rice hours before playing 90 minutes of football? I wasn't having it. Pasta and chicken would have been a good option but that stodgy rice was awful. The coach didn't seem to care and told us to eat it. I began to wonder, "Is this how it is?" I now see why some African nations are where they are in the football-ing world – the professionalism is just dire. You just don't eat a plate of oily rice three hours before a game of football.

That was followed by a bizarre turn of events. We were drawing the game 1-1 against Senegal and we started playing for the draw, thinking that would be enough to qualify us through to the finals. It's not in my nature to play for a draw – I wanted to win every game I played in – but the coach had decided a draw was enough. With that in mind, once the final whistle blew we all celebrated thinking we'd qualified – both teams celebrated in fact and most of the crowd from both sides ran onto the pitch. The heat was so stifling that some of us, including me, fell to the ground with exhaustion. I was completely dehydrated. The medics managed to recover my fluid levels and when I woke up I saw some fights kicking off inside and outside the stadium. It became so bad it was about six hours before we could leave the stadium and go back to the hotel. It was total chaos.

When we arrived back in Gambia, it seemed like the whole country had come to greet us at the airport. It was the first time Gambia had reached the finals of the African Cup of Nations – or so we thought. Even the President joined in and invited us to a party the next day at one of the small stadiums in the capital. A superb array of food and drink was laid on for us – it was fantastic.

Now, here's the kicker. The following day, we found out we hadn't qualified after all. Yes, that's right, CAF, the African Football Confederation, informed us that we didn't have enough points to qualify and the draw we had just played for wasn't actually good enough. When the news became public, the whole country went numb. I couldn't believe that nobody, particularly the coach, had checked the table before the game to consider the implications of playing for a draw. You just don't play for a draw – you've got to at least play to win the game.

Several weeks later, we had a double-header of friendlies in Germany and Portugal against Mexico and Angola, respectively. I was picked for the squad once more and travelled there for the games, but the coach put me on the bench for the Angola game. I didn't say anything to Paul and I didn't get a game. When we played Mexico, I was on the bench again – for the fourth time in a row. However, I did come on with about 20 minutes to go and made an immediate impact, setting up a goal when we were losing 5-1. If I remember rightly, Mexico had a decent line-up, which included Carlos Vela (Arsenal), Rafael Márquez (Barcelona) and Javier Hernández (Manchester United), who scored a hat-trick. Incidentally, I swapped my shirt with Márquez, so that made up for the result a little.

Even though I came on, I was livid about sitting on the bench for 70 minutes, so after the game I pulled Paul to one side and ranted at him, "Paul, what is your fucking problem? You're disrespecting me – you're really disrespecting me. What's going on? I'm not shit. I'm not shit. I've played in England – the greatest football country. You're trying to belittle me. I haven't come here to warm up your bench – you're taking the piss. I'm an experienced player and I'm a good player. Show me some respect. Don't take the piss. That's all I'm going to say." In reply, all he said was, "Yeah, I understand but it's just a tactical decision." By that time, I'd had enough and just before I left the room, I said, "Gambia have been after me for 15 years and you put me on the bench. Don't bring me here to warm your bench." We spoke about our differences for a few minutes then left it at that.

Pa Saikou Kujabi is a Gambian friend of mine who played in the same team as me for the national side. His nickname was 'Carlos', as he was built like Roberto Carlos, the Brazilian star – and because he was a left back. When I first met 'Carlos' in Gambia, the team were waiting for him on the bus, ready to go training one day, but he had a delayed journey from Austria. I was sitting at the back and I saw 'Carlos' running for the bus, so I asked one of the lads, "Who's that?" and he explained who it was. I looked at Carlos running and I said to my teammate, "Wow, I like him." There was something about him, maybe his physique, I don't know but he stood out and I liked his aura. When he got on board the bus he came straight to the back where I was sitting, we started talking and instantly hit it off. My immediate impression of him wasn't wrong because we became great mates from that day on.

After the game in Germany against Mexico, I went back with Pa Saikou to his house in Frankfurt, as he was playing for FSV Frankfurt at the time. We both had a few days off so spent most of that time talking about football and possible business ventures we were going to set up in Gambia, before I caught the train back to London, via Berlin. We stayed in close contact and he later left Frankfurt and came to the UK to play for Hibernian in Scotland during the 2012/2013 season. Pa Saikou has since retired from football and now lives in England, so we have become very close and see each other regularly in London.

During a training match before the following friendly game against Tunisia, Paul surprised me again because he told me I was playing and, not only that, but he asked me to play down the middle, rather than out wide. So during that game, I started to bang in the goals left, right and centre – doing what I do best. Surprisingly enough, I was picked for the squad for the game in Tunisia and he actually started me as promised. My rant must have worked!

The game was played on the eve of my 25th birthday. It was a friendly at the Stade el Menzah in Tunis on 9 January 2010.

I was fired up for the game and when I was singing the national anthem I felt very emotional indeed. Paul had partnered me up front with my pal, Ousman Jallow, but the first-half was dreadful and ended 0-0. Within 10 minutes of the re-start, we had the play on the left-hand side and a cross came in to the box from Sanna Nyassi and landed on my head as I dived to meet the ball. It was a terrific goal, even if I say so myself. Once I saw the ball in the back of the net, I jumped up, ran towards the corner flag and dropped to the ground and prayed to God, while all of my teammates piled on top of me. I started crying. It was a beautiful moment for me. It was a special goal for so many reasons; it was the eve of my birthday; it was my first start in a senior international game; I'd scored my first goal for Gambia, and to make things even better, we won the game 2-1. Not only that, I was happy because I'd got one over my coach. In fact, as the players were running back to the centre-circle to re-start the game, I made a point of running past the bench and winking at Paul. He winked back but I don't think he understood why I winked at him – I did it to show him, "Don't mess me about. This is what I can do." So, in that sense I had proved myself to him.

Come the next game, I felt I was odds-on to start again as I'd proved I was worthy of my starting place; however, he reverted back to putting me on the bench. I'd had enough of being messed about by him and I decided I would quit there and then. I made it clear to Paul that I was making myself unavailable for selection and told him not to call me up again. I couldn't even bear to find out why he'd benched me after scoring in the last game. That was it for me – I was done! In the back of my mind, I knew his motive and that I didn't figure in his plans, for whatever reason.

Paul was ultimately sacked shortly afterwards and I decided to make myself available again to the new manager.

I return to my old friend Mr Hindsight. Remember Michael Owen in World Cup '98 and the clamour of the English public and media for Glenn Hoddle to play him at the tender age of 18? Rather than shouting his mouth off and demanding to play due to public pressure, Michael sat in the background, quietly waited for his chance and got his rewards by scoring against Argentina. If I could turn back the clock now, maybe I would have handled the situation with Paul Put in a similar manner. However, at the time, the Gambian nation was clamouring for me to play. I was playing up to the demand and it rubbed off on me so I expected a starting place. It came to a stage when public pressure became too much to ignore and benching Cherno Samba became the unthinkable. Eventually, the pressure on Paul Put would have been too great – maybe the Gambian FA might have got involved – but in the end it all turned sour and I didn't bother to wait for that moment. Even when I scored and proved to him what I could do, I still didn't get the break and that was that.

Some years later, Paul got in touch and asked me if I could help him get a job at my old club in Greece – I don't need to tell you what I said to him.

As a so-called third-world nation, Gambia struggles to attract decent managers because of its low standing in the football world so the Gambian FA brought in Peter Bonu Johnson, a Gambian, for a short period then another third-rate manager, an Italian called Luciano Mancini, who couldn't even speak English. Oddly, Peter Bonu Johnson later became the assistant under Mancini. I worked under Mancini for a while and he was worse than Paul Put. He'd tell me to my face that I was going to start, but I'd later find out I was on the bench. He would also change his mind two or three times before making a decision whether to start me and I wasn't going to stand for that.

I was called up for a qualifier for the 2012 African Cup of Nations and Mancini told me I wasn't going to start, so I said I wasn't going to be on the bench and refused to play, but that I'd stay and watch the game from the stands before going back to England.

My Gambian journey was a beautiful one but ultimately a short one too, as that actually turned out to be the last time I was associated with the Gambian national side after just four appearances in the team.

Chapter 10

Racism Has No Place

"Not you Chern, you're one of us, mate"

Growing up in the environment I did, my parents prepared me well for life; however, I think racism is something I only discovered once I stepped outside the front door. My parents always prepared me for the fact that I don't look the same as the dominant race in this country. It's for that reason black people have to work harder, be better people, be stronger and come across better in order to succeed. It's part of a black person's life living in a country like England or the United States, or where being black isn't the dominant colour – it's just the way it is, I guess and I got used to it pretty quickly.

Seeing racism in football sadly isn't unusual and it didn't come as a surprise. Sometimes it's done quietly; it could come in a comment like someone using the word 'coloured', which is no longer politically correct, or it could be that someone is overlooked for a job. There are some black people who take offence and there are some, like me, who think, "Well, it is what it is," and try to move on.

However, there are times when people tip you over the edge, like the time I had an altercation with one of my teammates on the training ground in Spain. When I arrived at Cádiz, I was up against our star player, an Argentinian called Matías Pavoni. To be honest, I wanted to take his place in the side but the last thing he wanted was for someone like me to do that. It would soon become a problem – a black kid from England coming into the club wanting to take his position. I don't necessarily think it was because I was black – he didn't want anyone to take his place. However, I soon had an altercation with him when he called me a "black monkey" one day during training. He said that was because he knew I was faster than him and he thought it was ok for him to use that name. The saddest thing was that he had been saying it behind my back, until one day he couldn't hide his emotions and he just came out with it on the training ground, "Look at that black monkey run." I heard it loud and clear and by that time I'd had enough of it, so I went up to him and lashed out, but my teammates intervened. He'd insulted me by saying something racist – it wasn't as if I'd hit him for no reason. People may argue over whether he deserved it but I did what I did, rightly or wrongly in the heat of the moment.

The rest of the team all saw the incident and the training stopped immediately. Everyone backed me up and told Pavoni he shouldn't have said those things. When I'd calmed down, I told him, "Never, ever say that to me again. Next time I'll give you two punches." He never did say anything like that to me again, and ironically, we actually became good friends. I still think that he wasn't doing it to offend or upset me; he just didn't know any different. It was down to pure ignorance. While I don't condone violence, there are times when people push you over the edge and Matias had done just that.

People react differently to situations, but you can't tell someone how they should react to racism. When Danny Rose got abused on the pitch in an England Under-21 game away to Serbia in 2013, he reacted badly to the situation and was sent off. It must have been really bad for him to react in that way. In my view, the way to make a stand against racism is by walking off the pitch just like Kevin-Prince Boateng did when AC Milan played Pro Patria in a friendly game but, like I've said before, people react differently in the heat of the moment.

The punishments given out by FIFA or UEFA for racism reiterate how deep the problem is in football. As an example, a club gets fined £5,000 for racist chanting by so-called fans, which is a paltry sum. Their attitude towards racism and how it should be dealt with is to shake hands and move on, then give out a fine as a token gesture. It seems like the football authorities don't take it seriously. As in life, racism in football is ignorance – sad but true. If you get too caught up in trying to deal with it, you can take your eye off your real focus and end up being quite hateful. You can't counteract hate with hate; you've just got to keep on moving. As a footballer, you need to ignore it and get on and focus on your own game, but it doesn't always go that way.

Fortunately, I have never been on the wrong end of pure racism in English football. That's not to say it doesn't exist, but I have only experienced it from a distance once and that was when I was sitting in the stands at The Den. I was watching a game as I was injured and I witnessed a Millwall fan sitting just behind me shouting out some obscenities at two or three black players on the opposition team. When I heard it, I turned round to look at the guy and stared at him. He spotted me, waved and shouted with a smile on his face, "Not you Chern. You're one of us mate. You're one of us..." and carried on with his abuse of the opposition. I can smile about it now, but I'll never forget that incident. Even though it was aimed at the opposing players and not me, it was still an act of misguided bigotry and ignorance.

Although racism is much better in the English game compared to the 1970s and 1980s, it remains a big problem in European football. In my experience of some European countries, Spain especially, it's rife. The racism I was subjected to really didn't bother me and, in fact, it only gave me more motivation to do even better. Don't get me wrong, it was hard to deal with and when I did complain to the referee or officials, there was no back up – nothing was done about it, so I thought, "What's the point in protesting?"

I remember we (England) played in Poland at Under-19 level and Anton Ferdinand and I were the only black players on the pitch. The Polish fans were very harsh and screamed monkey noises at us every time we kicked the ball. It was far from the friendly match it was meant to be, but we carried on as if nothing had happened.

We were in a hotel restaurant in Hungary before another friendly when a group having dinner and another guest refused to enter because I was there, the only black person in the restaurant. When we heard about it, I walked out and went upstairs to my room. It was outrageous behaviour but it demonstrates the problem some of these countries have. In that situation, I think I made the right decision.

When I was living in Spain, I remember a group of kids spotting me in the street and saying to their parents something like, "Hay una persona negro," which in English translates to "There's a black person." Another time, I was walking down a street in Málaga when some kids spoke to their Mum and then ran up to me and said (in Spanish), "Can I see your skin?" So I put my arm out and the kids started stroking it. Then the kids said, "Muy bien," which means "Very nice." Their Mum came up to me and apologised, which was fine by me, but the kids stood there still stroking my skin like they were stroking a dog. When they'd had enough of stroking my arm, I asked their mum to teach them that some people have different coloured skin, because it was obvious they hadn't seen another black person before. I guess it might be the same for me if I saw a blue person for the first time? That type of thing happened a few times and, while I didn't think that was pure racism as such or something that made me feel uncomfortable, it did strike me that those kids simply didn't know any differently and I guess you'd just call it ignorance.

It's all about a lack of education, in my opinion. While those kids never bothered me in the slightest, there are some people who are racist and ignorant of the facts.

One night, Fes and I, together with another 15 black guys, went to a nightclub in Málaga for Fes's stag party. In the club, we walked past a group of Spanish guys and one of them called out, "Nigger..." The lads (except me, of course) had all been drinking for a while, but as soon as we heard that we chased those bigots out of the nightclub and through the town until we finally caught up with them. One of our friends, Darran Weston, who was generally a cool guy and would never lose his temper, flipped out at these Spanish guys – I'd never seen him in that state before. You just cannot and should not say that word to a black guy. They soon realised how serious we were and bizarrely, the guy who'd shouted the comment actually got beaten up by one of his own friends. I guess it was a choice between that or them all getting beaten up by us – either way, that bigot got his comeuppance.

In the dressing room, racism goes on all the time, especially in Spain. Not only was I a foreigner, but also I was a black guy, so I really copped it – those two things counted against me in Spain. At first, I couldn't speak Spanish but after eight months I learned the language. I don't think the lads knew I could speak Spanish almost fluently by this point and that I was able to understand everything that was said. What they said was hurtful and also went against any team ethics. They said things like, "Don't pass to the black guy..." Normally, I'd just brush it off and ignore it, but what they were doing was intentionally not passing to me because of my colour. As time went on, I'd say something in return to lighten the mood, like, "No, no pass to the black kid..."

I didn't complain to the coaches, as that would be considered weak and not cool, so I just got on with it. I thought that my personality and skills on the pitch would eventually shine through and they would see past the colour of my skin. I saw it as a case of me having to prove myself as a player to gain their respect; it didn't take me long to show that I could play a bit and they soon started passing the ball to me.

It was the same during away games in Spain. The fans used to chant things like, "black monkey" and I'd hear monkey noises in the stands and they also threw bananas at me. That also happened when I played in Norway and Finland later in my career. It was 'normal' in those countries. None of those things ever distracted me from my game and at no time did those fans ever mess with my head either. In fact, the more they shouted things from the stands, the more it motivated me to do well on the pitch. To overcome those sorts of things you need to have mental strength and I had that in abundance.

Racism affects people differently and it also affects families. I remember watching Samuel Eto'o play for Barcelona at Real Zaragoza in February 2005 when Zaragoza supporters began making racist taunts and monkey-like chants whenever he had possession of the ball. However, the referee made no mention of the incidents in his match report, commenting only that the behaviour of the crowd was "normal". Infuriated again by Zaragoza fans' racist chants the following season, Samuel attempted to walk off the pitch in protest but his teammates intervened and convinced him to continue playing. He was constantly subject to racism in Spain and Italy and it affected him and his family badly to the point where I think he stopped his family going to watch him play in the end.

I actually met Samuel Eto'o when we played Barcelona at the La Rosaleda and I was watching Málaga 'A' team before we played our own 'B' team game. I bumped into him and he called me over, probably because I was the only black person in our team. When we met, he greeted me by holding my shoulder and asking me where I was from, "I'm from England," I said. "No, no where are you from originally?" he asked. Again, I said I was from England and for the third time he asked me again, "Where were you born and where are your parents from?" I finally answered him by saying I was from The Gambia. He then asked me how I was settling into life in Spain and whether I'd come across any racism. He was great to talk to and offered to help me if I needed anything. He even gave me his phone number. Wow! Samuel Eto'o gave me his mobile number! He also gave me his shirt after the game and he had mine in exchange. I guess he understood what it was like being a black person in Spain and I appreciated the chat we had. It was very nice.

Certain parts of Spain are worse than others when it comes to racism. Málaga was so different from Cádiz in terms of the type of racism I encountered. I remember one night Angerine and I went out to dinner at the Chinese restaurant, which was located underneath my apartment, and it was packed with locals. There was only one remaining table and it was next to us, so anyone who came in had to sit there. The problem was nobody wanted to sit there so, after a while, the waiters took the table and chairs outside so people would occupy the table. Angerine started crying and she told me she was home-sick and wanted to go back to London. I tried to explain to her that some people are not educated and in fact most of the locals probably hadn't seen a black person in their lives. It was at that point that I did something so random and off-the-wall. I stood up from our table inside the restaurant, took my plate of food and sat myself down in an unoccupied seat next to the couple that had refused to sit by us. Then I started eating my food with my hands. My aim was to piss them off. I got some funny looks from the other customers but I went back inside after a few minutes. I guess I just wanted to make a point to those ignorant people, but I admit it was a pretty random act. However, Angerine felt really uncomfortable and was still crying, so I went back in and explained to her that it was "just part of life in Spain..." She told me there and then that she couldn't take it anymore and didn't want to be a part of it. It wasn't the cleverest thing I'd ever done and I guess it wasn't the correct way to react either, but it was the only thing I could think of at the time.

That episode in the restaurant put some pressure on me because I had two years left on my contract. However, shortly after we left that restaurant, we decided our Spanish adventure was over and planned for life back home in London. I'd put my family before my work and I saw it as the only thing I could do. I thought about the bigger picture and asked myself whether I wanted my children to be brought up in that sort of environment. The answer was, "No."

Sometimes, things get so bad that you just can't tolerate it anymore and my experience of racism in a country like Finland was really awful – worse than in Spain, in fact. It was so bad that I only lasted six months of an 18-month contract and it got to the stage where I just couldn't take any more. There was only one other black person in the Haka squad – a Nigerian boy called Abdullahi Ishaka – and we shared a house together. The players at FC Haka wouldn't speak to us at first and didn't share anything with us. They would talk about us behind our backs and it was so bad that they even refused to pass the ball to us. It became a real problem. I'd experienced racism before in Europe but the type of personal torture we faced was just too much so I decided I didn't want to stay, even though the money they offered was decent. Money is one thing but I hated the place and just couldn't hack it.

When you consider a third of all professional footballers in England are black, that's disproportionately higher than the amount of black people in the country, which is around 3.5%. In football management, you can count on one hand the amount of black coaches in England; that tells its own story. However, the FA coaching courses are full of black people trying to progress into coaching or management, which says to me the FA are proactively trying to address the imbalance between black and white coaches. Ex-Arsenal player Paul Davis told me recently that the chances of black players becoming coaches in England are higher now than they have ever been because the FA are actively pushing and encouraging black players into coaching, and that can only be a good thing – it's a start anyway.

In the football world, I really think racism is a problem in terms of certain levels of job, although in recent times it has improved with the likes of Paul Ince, Chris Hughton, Chris Powell and Chris Ramsey being given high-profile management jobs in club football. There is still a lack of black coaches in England and I think one reason is that some black former players simply don't believe they will be given a fair chance to prove they can become top coaches or take on top jobs – and that is wrong.

To put it into context, there are so many black coaches who have been trying to put me off becoming a coach, saying things like, "You're a black man. You've got no chance at being a coach." Well, I don't follow that logic because while black ex-footballers continue to have that belief, then, we as black men won't break that mould. I intend to help change people's attitudes and mind-set on that front.

In the United States, their way of addressing racism is something called the 'Rooney Rule', which requires every NFL team to interview at least one black person for any coaching job that is advertised, whether they are good enough or not. The idea is that this increases the chances of a black person being hired for that job. In early 2018, the English FA introduced its own version of the Rooney Rule into English football and I, for one, couldn't be happier. I've always had a feeling that things would change and I'm pleased to say the FA are trying to do everything possible to alter the status quo and make sure everyone has an equal opportunity. The introduction of the rule will give black coaches more of a chance to get a job but it's not a guarantee that any black person will actually get it; it's only right that the job should go to the best person, whether they are white, black, yellow or blue. Everyone must prove themselves regardless of colour and race and if you're good enough you'll stand a better chance. Time will tell whether this is actually a positive move, but it's certainly a very good step in the right direction. What it shows is that football has come a long way since the 1970s and for someone like me, there's no better time to be a black coach.

Being a successful coach doesn't come naturally to some, regardless of race or colour. You can be one of the greatest players and not be a successful coach. The difference being, the white coaches keep being given chance after chance – and still fail. Maybe that tells you why there are so many foreign coaches in the English leagues, because our coaches aren't good enough? The question of whether black players are good enough to be coaches is irrelevant considering the number of white ones out there who have proven not to be up to scratch. So black players can't be any worse, can they? Yet they aren't being given enough opportunities. There needs to be a greater balance. If you're good enough, black or white, you should be given a chance, simple as that.

We have to change the mentality so that some black people begin to believe they will be given a fair crack, rather than having a negative view that being black will count against them. It's not for me to judge whether particular people are right or wrong with their views, but my ambition and my goal is to try and become a coach. I want to learn my trade and go through it the hard way so that, one day, I get to the top. My philosophy is that if I prove to be good enough because of my skills and experience then, with a bit of luck, I will be given an opportunity regardless of the colour of my skin – that's my definition of fairness.

Chapter 11
Too Much, Too Young

"You can be the next Dele Alli...."

Looking back on my life and knowing what I know now, in a funny way I wish I'd had the opportunity to begin my football career in Spain because I really believe it would have turned out very differently. I'd have learned a lot more about 'real life' and how to work hard for my money. Unfortunately, like most kids coming through the ranks in England's top clubs, I had everything given to me on a plate and I thought money grew on trees.

Some footballers these days seem to have inflated egos and a level of arrogance about them from such a young age that didn't seem to exist in players of yesteryear. I think the main reason is they're in the public eye constantly. From a young age, their innocence is taken away from them because of their fame and fortune and that's not a good thing. It must be difficult for young players these days to turn down the amounts of money and the publicity they receive. I know that to be true because I've been there, done it and bought the (designer) t-shirt.

By the time those lads reach the age of 21 and have developed to a decent level, some of them probably won't even care about the football and are more interested in the amount of money in their bank account or the cars they drive. Every Tom, Dick or Harry wants a piece of them and it must be tempting to take everything on offer – it certainly was for me. There's no shame in thinking, "I'm on the front of the newspaper – I'm good and I've made it." I thought I'd made it when I was about to sign for Liverpool. Why would you doubt whether you're going to make it to the top if you see yourself in the headlines every day?

Then, you have agents and advisors telling lads the things they want to hear so as not to upset their prized assets. As a youngster, you only want to hear that you're good and you're going to make it to the big time. Those things can affect people in different ways and it's potentially very damaging, especially if they don't end up making it in football. Players these days have to be very grounded and strong to see through the smokescreen but at that age you know nothing about life.

When my move to Liverpool fell through at the age of 15, the club probably thought I was just another youngster to slip through the net, but for me it was my life and it hit me really hard. As I've said before, it affected me big time because the whole episode made me fall out of love with football and I ended up staying away from the game for six months or so. It affected me in other ways too. I began to doubt my ability as a footballer and I lost the appetite for the game. Fortunately, my family supported me and encouraged me to go back to Millwall.

When it comes to blame, it's difficult because I can't blame Millwall as they were only looking after their own interests and my own people were trying to do the best for me. I can't say anything bad about Millwall because it was my club and I grew up there. For sure, I was swayed by the headlines about me and I was swallowed up in all the hype about my move to one of the biggest clubs in the world – it was hard not to be and for that I can only blame myself. Maybe my own ego got the better of me. I say that because I should have been stronger and realised that things like that happen in football from time-to-time – everyone gets disappointments at some point in their career, but I didn't know anything else as a 15-year-old. It's the same in 'real life', too. Maybe I should have looked myself in the mirror and asked, "What could I have done better?" In football, you have to buckle down, listen to the right people and work hard, or you don't get on. You could have all the talent in the world but it won't get you anywhere unless you work hard. If I'd have done those things, I would have got to where I wanted to be – at the top playing for Liverpool in the Premier League. Unfortunately, I did the opposite.

I would like to be able to think football had moved on since the year 2000 but in my opinion it hasn't – in fact I think it's gone the other way and players haven't learned from stories like mine. My story is just one of many, I'm afraid.

We're now in a climate where there are hundreds of players out of contract in England and half of them are under 23 years old, which is a worrying statistic. Of course, the influx of foreign players has had a huge impact but it seems that football in England is still all about money and you'll find that some of the players we have here are only motivated by the vast amounts of cash on offer. Money may be "the root of all evil," but it also "makes the world go round." In modern day football, there's no happy medium.

Take Jesse Lingard, for example, whom I think is a good player. He's a Manchester United squad player and went from picking up a five-figure sum each week to a (reported) six-figure sum each week and it was highlighted in the media for days. He's lucky to be at one of the biggest clubs in the world. As I understand it, he's a hardworking lad, but he has a long way to go before he can say he is a great player. He has raw talent at the moment but he has the potential to be a great player one day if he works hard and makes the right decisions. In a team like United you need players like Jesse – you don't need 11 superstars. However, my point is what sort of example does that set to everyone else? "Jesse did it, so I can do it."

There are exceptions; somebody like Dele Alli, whom I rate highly and reminds me of a young Paul Gascoigne – he's got 'it'. I would say there are probably ten players in the Premier League who are exceptions to the rule and those are the ones you hear about, week-in, week-out. Harry Kane is another. While those players' names get bigger and bigger, the lads coming through the ranks at the same clubs will be saying, "That can be me one day" or an agent approaches them and will claim, "You can be the next Dele Alli".

Here's what I'd be saying if I was their agent – "Rather than being the next Dele Alli, why don't you be the next YOU?" My advice would be to take your time and be patient because you can make a great living from football anyway. Forget the 'exceptions', they're an anomaly, so concentrate on yourself.

Football is lucky to have exceptional talents like Lionel Messi and Cristiano Ronaldo, but before they graced the football field there were a batch of 'superstars', including the likes of Ronaldinho, Romário, Ronaldo (the original), Zidane, Beckham, Roberto Carlos, Figo – the list goes on. All those were 'world-class' players but now the whole world goes crazy about basically two players. Yes, it's good to see these guys as examples of 'world class' but the point I'm making is when agents take young players and say things like, "You're going to take England to the 2006 World Cup," it becomes a problem. That is what everyone said to me when I was 17 and living on a council estate in Camberwell. I believed the hype and was heartbroken when it didn't happen for me.

What football needs right now are people to keep these young prospects under wraps a little bit and to say to them, "That's all well and good, but you're not there yet. Let's earn the right to be there." The media don't help in raising players' profiles and that feeds into the hands of the agents. Football is a business, which can be fine, but it also breaks lives as well. So many kids are left heartbroken and that's why we need some reality put back into the world of football. Kids these days are told they will make a decent living and have a solid career playing in the Championship or League One. Added to that is the prospect of playing abroad – in China, for example – which is where the new money is. Everybody wants to get to the top, but not all players can, so the ones who don't are left devastated.

Some of the biggest issues we have in the game are to do with the players themselves and their own image and egos. I really believe that our players look at each other, compare what other players have, what clothes their peers wear and what cars they drive. By doing that, they feel they have to follow suit and find themselves buying the designer clothes and the flash cars, just to keep up with their peers. It seems that everyone is in competition with each other's image nowadays, rather than competing on the pitch. I can relate to that because when I was 17 years old I bought a brand new Peugeot 206 worth £11,000, simply because all of my peers were buying cars. At the time it was 'the car' to have and I paid cash for it. That was a significant amount of money but it goes to show what was on offer to me. A few years later, when I was at Plymouth, I bought my dream car – an expensive top-of-the-range BMW 3-Series – again because all the others guys had a flash car and I wanted to keep up with them. Then I look at all those trips to Nike Town where I'd spend thousands of pounds in a single shopping trip. It's easy for me to reflect on it now, but it's really hard when you're not experienced in life.

From my own experiences, things seem slightly different abroad. The philosophy regarding young players is really different to the way we treat our young footballers in England – and it's quite refreshing. Regardless of who you are, you're paid according to your personal situation. They see young players as having no responsibilities in life so the older you are, the better you get paid. If you're young, you don't need 20,000 Euros a week. When I was playing in La Liga, status didn't matter and young players were even expected to take their boots and kit home to clean. It all made perfect sense to me. For example, as a teenager you could be playing week in, week out in La Liga and you might be earning 2,000 Euros per month. Alternatively, as a 29 year old, you could be earning 18,000 Euros per week and not playing in the first team regularly. It means if you're married with kids, you get paid more but young teenage players are given just enough to live on as they suspect most young players will be living with their parents so have no financial burden. That obviously doesn't happen here.

With the exception of maybe a handful of players who like to have a certain image to keep intact, Spanish players don't seem to be money hungry and don't seem give a toss about any of the material things. Knowing that when I was playing there sort of relaxed me, and I could turn up to training wearing anything I liked. In fact, someone even turned up in pyjamas one day – seriously! Some of my teammates, including the top class players, drove around in 'ordinary' cars but no one looked at them any differently. I really respected that attitude and still do. If you walked into any training round in England wearing slippers or pyjamas, you'd get caned. Similarly, if you turned up in a Ford Fiesta you'd be laughed out of town. That sort of mentality we have in our game doesn't help our players, young or old. In fact, it doesn't help anybody because you're not being yourself and you start living a false life, living a lie, and that's no good for anyone.

Unlike here in England, the Spanish don't tend to hype up their young players. In fact, I have an example of a player who came to Spain from Paraguay aged 15 at around the same time that I joined Cádiz. When I first saw him, I thought he was unbelievable – mesmerising, in fact. He was in the same mould as Sergio Agüero – really strong, fast and sharp. The lad was kept away from the spotlight because in Spain the clubs would rather make them work hard for several years until they are ready, both as a person and as a player.

Sure, that philosophy may make the player feel like they are somehow less worthy, but it's the best way to look after young players. Now, if he was an English player or he had come to the English Premier League instead, he would have been all over the media in no time. Spanish clubs don't boost their egos and hype them up in the media after one fantastic game in the reserves like we do in England. By working the kids hard and making them realise they will get to where they want to be if they buckle down and follow their clubs' instructions, it's a brilliant way to manage them. The FA should take note.

Now, compare that scenario to the hype that the latest 'wonder kid', Karamoko Dembele from Celtic is getting. The country went wild over the 13-year old lad and everyone knew about him in no time because he was all over social media and in the national press. Sure, he looks the part and he made his debut for Celtic Under-20s at the start of the 2016/2017 season, seven years above his own age group, but the sad thing is Karamoko is no longer a kid who wants to play football for fun. He's become 'a commodity'. It's a fantastic achievement in itself for the lad to be recognised in that light but watching it from a distance brought back memories of when the exact same thing happened to me at a similar age. It's just not healthy. It's ok for football to be a business, but within that you still need kids to be grounded and prepared for potential failure, as well as stardom. That's why you need people around these young kids to advise them properly. Let them enjoy themselves and enjoy their football – once they start doing it at the highest level, then we can start talking them up. For me, it's not right at the moment.

I really think that things will only get worse while the huge amounts of money remain on offer and that's a sad state of affairs if you ask me. Football's a crazy industry and everyone is wondering where it will all end and when or if the bubble will burst, because it's just not sustainable. Fortunately, there are positive moves being made by the FA and some football clubs. We've seen recently that some of the top clubs in England, Liverpool being one, have introduced wage caps for young players. This can only be a good thing and every club should follow suit. Personally, I think it has come too late – it should have happened 10 or 15 years ago. While there are multi-million pound TV deals in football and a worldwide audience, nothing will change, but who am I to argue?

I'm just another talented ex-player who fell through the net at a young age, giving my own opinion about the game I love.

Chapter 12

Cherno Samba –
Championship Manager 'Legend'

"You're THE Cherno Samba? The one
from Championship Manager?"

For those who don't know anything about computer games, *Football Manager* was a series of football management simulation games that began its life in 1992 as *Championship Manager*; however, it was re-branded in 2004 to *Football Manager* with a new publisher, Sega.

When we first became aware of *Championship Manager*, I remember David Bentley saying to me, "Bloody hell, I can't afford you, Cherno. You need to lower your wage demands." I used to have a laugh with him about it and said I didn't know what he was talking about. That was around the time I was the next 'wonderkid' on the block in the real football world and everyone wanted a piece of a player who was, "set to win the World Cup for England in 2006".

Unbeknown to me, I was also the next 'wonderkid' in the virtual world, too.

When I was a 13-year-old at Millwall, some of my mates came up to me and asked if I knew about the new computer game. "You're amazing on it", they said, so I went away and looked it up, got Mum to buy the game and started to play

Championship Manager for myself. I thought it was so weird, seeing myself on a computer game, but it was something unbelievable at the same time. The way they made me in that game was incredible – if only I had turned out like that in reality.

Before I announced my retirement from real football at the age of 29, it could be said that I had become more famous for my 'legendary' status on *Championship Manager*. I was attributed scores that reflected my ability and potential to become one of the world's best virtual footballers. When gamers booted up the 2001/2002 version of the game, made a beeline for a young, cheap Cherno Samba, and then sat back, I apparently fired thousands of them to virtual glory. As my real career almost wasted away, my name was reverberating around halls of residence and student bars all over the country. Arguably my impressive in-game stats enabled my virtual presence to overtake my real life football career.

Everyone who has played *Championship Manager* probably has their own 'Cherno Samba story' and perhaps it's a far more personal one than they might have had if they had actually known me. The virtual me would have been unfazed at the prospect of becoming your first-choice striker at 16 years old and being the guaranteed bail-out option to take you exactly where you wanted to be, regardless of your team's level, while usually finding the time to take England to 2006 and 2010 World Cup glory, too. I was the greatest English footballer of my generation, but only on the hugely popular computer simulation game.

However, it is the switching between fantasy and reality that has given the game its allure over the years and created its 'legends', including me. My American equivalent, Freddie Adu, was also something of a cult hero in *Championship Manager* and our own characteristics were attributed to real, visible evidence of our own potential from where anything could have happened – and often did. If either of us had enjoyed something close to our projected career potential, then the satisfaction and amusement would have been far less in taking our virtual selves to heights that even Messi or Ronaldo could barely envisage. For me, as a virtual player I went from prodigal teenager at Millwall to a goalscoring machine at the top level, a guaranteed 25-goal-a-season striker, but in reality my career didn't turn out like that.

It is a curious thought that, while my own potential led to those heady computer game exploits, my high-profile presence on the game may to some extent have helped me maintain my career as a player. The notion of a *'Championship Manager* Legend' may lead us to marvel at the short leap from actuality to imagination, but it also prompts the thought that success and failure are not always what they seem, either.

For a long time, I was haunted by the discrepancy between my abilities in *Championship Manager* and my record in real life. Opposition defenders would sometimes taunt me about it. It was so bad that for years I denied I played the computer game, even though I did, while my legend continued to spread with the young people who stayed up all night playing it. I soon started realising I was big in this thing. They'd made me the best in the world. People would come up to me, and say, "Listen, mate, I'm a big fan of you in *Championship Manager,"* and they'd take a picture of me. That was nice and made me feel good, but then there were lots of fellow players who were fans of the game – I've been at clubs where all they talked about was *Championship Manager*. When I was at Plymouth, one day in training I shot well wide, and Barry Hayles, said: "F**king hell, Cherno. That's not why I bought you in *Championship Manager."* So I started pretending I didn't play it. It just got too much.

Having said all of that, I'm very grateful to the makers of the game, Sports Interactive and Sega, that my name has been associated with it for such a long time because I've had some great stories on the back of my virtual fame. When I was particularly popular, my mobile phone provider once cut the delivery time from 3 months to a next-day delivery when I told the phone agent that he was serving Cherno Samba. To his amazement, he replied with, "You're THE Cherno Samba? The one from *Championship Manager*?" Sometimes, these things go in your favour when you least expect them to.

There was another story that I've already covered in the book, when I was detained at Heathrow on my return from Iran. A policewoman happened to recognise me and told her colleagues, "That's Cherno Samba – my son plays him on *Championship Manager*" and we ended up having pictures taken together. It lightened the mood significantly following an hour's worth of questioning by Her Majesty's officials.

Even after 12 years, people still talk to me about the game and how well I played for them – or not. Most people still know me as a 'legend' of *Championship Manager / Football Manager* and it's nice to make people happy. I must admit I'm very pleased to have been associated with the game and, if anything, it has enhanced my name and reputation. Credit is due to the makers of the game and to the fans that played it. As a concept and as a vehicle for me, the involvement I've had with the game has been immeasurable and they have been amazing to me.

When *Football Manager 2017* was released, I was lucky enough to be at the forefront of an integrated marketing campaign for TV, online, advertising, print and social media, with the TV ads aired on Sky Sports from October until Christmas 2016. I was seen in the TV advert playing pool and it featured creative gamers playing the game on the move, at home and even at a live football match. Even an old Panini sticker of me in a Millwall kit appeared somewhere in the advert. Some people said it was the best *Football Manager* advert yet, and that's great news for the game.

I love the fact that I now have a working relationship with its makers, 15 years after I was made famous. There's even talk of me working with them again in the near future, which would be great. Having met the guys at Football Manager, they are a great bunch of people who are extremely passionate and proud of their product. They are all knowledgeable about the game and clever and sophisticated enough to know it is about more than just football.

I'm also very grateful to the fans because without them there wouldn't be a game and I wouldn't have been so popular. When I'm 75 years old, I bet people will still be talking to me about it and that's remarkable, really.

What would be really cool would be to get myself, Freddie Adu and Tonton Zola Moukoko doing some sort of promo for a future release of the game – now imagine that advert. It would be insane!

We'll see what happens. You never know.

Chapter 13

My OCD

"Samba, what is wrong with you?"

Those who know me personally are aware that I have a condition called Obsessive Compulsive Disorder (OCD). It is a mental health disorder that affects people of all ages in all walks of life and it occurs when a person gets caught in a cycle of obsessions and compulsions. Obsessions are unwanted, intrusive thoughts, images or urges that trigger intensely distressing feelings. In my case, my obsession is cleanliness.

OCD is nothing to feel ashamed or embarrassed about. It's a health condition like any other – it doesn't mean you're "mad" and it's not your fault if you have it.

I believe it started when I was aged about ten or so, helping my Mum in the house when she did the cleaning. I used to help do the chores, the cleaning and tidying up every day. It's unusual for someone so young to be so clean and house proud, but I was different to the rest of the kids and I didn't think anything of it at the time.

The first time I realised it was affecting me (and affecting other people) was just after we'd bought our home in Plymouth. We had white carpets throughout the house, a white sofa and a white kitchen. Having a white carpet meant that everybody who came to our house had to take off their shoes, which isn't so bad in itself and I'd guess is quite normal. For some reason, I just love white things – but I hate dirt and dirty things. I don't know why I like white so much; all of my trainers are white and as soon as they get dirty, I throw them away – I don't even clean them, I just buy a new pair. I just don't think they're ever the same again. It sounds really wasteful, I know, but that's just the way I am.

Our first child was born in 2006 and when we fed her, I used to put loads of sheets down on the carpet beneath her highchair in the middle of the living room so she could make a mess on the sheets rather than on the white carpet. When she'd finished eating, I'd take the sheets from away and throw them in the bin – I didn't even wash them, I just chucked them away. I bought loads of sheets, so nothing was recycled or reused. Looking back, it was such a waste, but now we have a new baby daughter I'm finding myself doing the same thing again. Nothing has changed, it seems.

It was around this time that I was diagnosed with OCD by the doctor. I was getting anxious about my compulsive behaviour so he gave me some tablets to try and control the anxiety. The tablets actually made it worse at the beginning, but after a while it controlled things a little. Along with the tablets, I went to see a therapist, but I don't really think that did any good. I remember the doctor telling me I had to sort it out otherwise it would have a big impact on my life – and it did, big time.

It began affecting other people too. When Fes came to the house, he'd try and wind me up by touching my clothes; I hate people going through my things, so I got annoyed with him and it caused so many arguments between us. At the time, he didn't realise I had OCD and just thought he was having a laugh.

Even worse, my compulsions nearly ruined my marriage. Angerine just couldn't take it at first and she had to get used to my ways pretty quickly and it was hard for her to adjust.

I have very firm routines in my life. I have to iron all my clothes, even my underwear, and put my clothes away in a certain way. Not only that, but when my clothes have been ironed and I'm going out, my clothes have to be placed on the bed in a certain way. First my trousers are laid out, then my shirt, boxers and socks – in that order. Now, that's not 'normal' is it? Even cleaning my teeth is a chore because it may take me about 45 minutes – can you believe that? I'll probably repeat the routine about three or four times. I constantly doubt that my teeth and my mouth are clean, but again, it's all in my head.

It makes me frustrated and sometimes angry that I'm like this. For most men, it may take half an hour to have a shower and get changed when they go out, but for me it may take three times as long. God help me if I'm out and I see a stain on my clothes, as I automatically think I need to get changed. Sometimes it's not possible, but usually I will go home and change my shirt or something.

I'd go so far as to say that cleanliness rules my life. I shower three or four times every single day and I'm normally in the shower for 45 minutes. I keep scrubbing myself over and over again, thinking that I'm not clean enough. When I come in from a day out or from training, the first thing I do is to wash my hands and then have a shower. Even more anal, when I touch something when I'm out, I have to wash my hands straight away. I also hate crumbs being dropped on the floor in the house. Fes used to wind me up over this too, as he'd drop crumbs on the carpet just to irritate me and I would always have to hoover up the crumbs straight away.

In the kitchen, all the food products are lined up in order, so all the tins of beans are together, all the tins of tuna are together and so on. I hate gaps in the cupboards or in the fridge – I have to fill them with something, so I go shopping and stock up the shelves. It really irritates me to see gaps – it drives me crazy. If a bottle of water is drunk and a gap appears in the fridge, I will go out specifically and buy some more bottled water in order to fill the gap. I know that sounds really stupid, but it's one of my many quirks. Not only that, but the bottles have to be put in the fridge or cupboard in a certain way; as does all the crockery, the cups, plates and dishes. I don't have to tell you that the kitchen cupboards are white and all of the crockery is white – it must be another obsession. Honestly, it's just mad, but I can't help it. I know it's all in my head.

The kitchen cupboards in our house are always spotless because I'm constantly cleaning them, inside and out. Yes, the cupboards are white and it's a colour that gets dirty easily, but still I'm forever cleaning the shelves and cupboard doors. I'll do it over and over again, every single day. Then there's the floor, I could stay there all day mopping the kitchen floor, even though it looks spotless to most people.

Washing up is also a big thing for me. When someone leaves even a few bits of food on their plate, instead of knocking them off into the sink I make sure every bit of food goes into the bin before I clean the plate. I hate food going into the sink, even the tiniest molecule – it drives me crazy. When someone washes up and leaves drops of water in the sink or on the draining board, I hate that too. If I'm washing up, I have to wipe the surfaces dry and don't leave any drops of water anywhere. If someone else washes up, I will go round and dry the surfaces. Angerine goes mad when I do this and says, "Do you know when you wash up, the water has to touch the sink?"

It's not just my own house that I clean, though. When I go to other people's houses, and find some dirt or drops of water in the sink, I have to clean it up. I remember at Toby's house in Liverpool, he'd had a shower and went into his bedroom to get changed, so I quickly dashed into the bathroom and cleaned the bath free from drops of water. I think he thought I was mental when he saw me cleaning up after him. He said, "Cherno, it's a bath tub and it usually has water in it". So, it not only affects me in my own home, it affects me in other people's houses too. If ever I see untidiness, I will go round and clean up, regardless of where I am.

Not everyone is as lenient and accommodating of my obsessions as Toby was. In fact, it got so bad with one person that I lost his friendship because of my compulsions. I drove from Plymouth to London to see a mate and when I got to his house, I saw he was such a messy guy so I started tidying up – while he was at the shops. I tidied up the kitchen, the toilet and rearranged most of his house by the time he came back. When he saw what I'd done, he went mad and told me to get out of his house, so I left. I called him on my way home and apologised but he wouldn't have any of it. To this day, we still don't talk to each other.

Nobody likes making the bed, but for me it's a real chore because it takes around 20 minutes. Every sheet and duvet cover has to be ironed and when I make the bed it looks immaculate. What disturbs me is when someone sits on the bed or has a lie down on the bed, which means the sheets get creased. So, when I get the opportunity I strip the bed, iron the sheets and make the bed again. Not to mention the pillows and the cushions – they have to be ordered in a certain way on the bed, too. Fes will deliberately jump on the bed just to muck the bed sheets up so I have to go through the routine of ironing them again and then remake the bed. It drives me nuts and he knows it. It's such a waste of time, but what can I do?

When our kids play in the house, I'm watching them all the time, thinking about the mess they make with their toys. As soon as they have finished playing I'm cleaning up their mess – I know I shouldn't but I just hate mess in the house. When I'm at home, all I seem to do is clean up, and I'd go as far to say I'm possessed with cleanliness. Angerine knows how bad my problem is and she will clean up before I arrive home, just to stop me moaning and insisting on cleaning up before I do anything else, which causes arguments between us. Even though Angerine tidies up immaculately, nobody can do it the way I do, so I'll probably end up doing it all again. That says it all for me.

Every time I go out, there is a routine I go through that drives me, and everyone else, nuts. Most people lock up their house, jump in the car and drive off, but I will go through that routine maybe twice or three times. I will lock up the house, go and sit in the car, and then think, "Have I locked up properly?" and then go to check the front door again. This will happen several times before I eventually drive away.

Cleanliness also rules in my car and I don't let anyone eat or drink in it. Obviously, it's white and anyone who comes in my car thinks it's brand new as it's so clean, inside and out. Even in restaurants, if I see someone leave their plates on the table, I will go over to the table and clean up after them. My eldest daughter said to me recently, "Daddy, what are you doing? It's not ours, leave it there". I was so embarrassed that I came back and sat down like a naughty schoolboy!

I'm not just freaky about cleanliness. Whenever someone comes to our house, whoever it is, if they are slouching or sitting on the edge of the sofa, I will ask them to sit properly. Now, that goes beyond compulsion.

When I was playing football, I'd always change my kit at half time, but I think a lot of players do that anyway. Sometimes, players would sit and rest up for a few minutes or have a chat about the game, but I only had one thing on my mind – to get out of my dirty kit and get cleaned up in the shower.

While I was playing in Spain, I think my teammates thought I was crazy. When I got changed before a game, I had a routine where I'd hang my clothes in a certain order. I would hang my boxers first, then my trousers, then put my shirt on a hanger and if I had a jacket, that would go over the top of the shirt – in that order. However, the rest of the lads weren't so anal and would simply hang their clothes in any old fashion.

I'd rearrange the clothes of the player next to me in the same order that I had mine. My teammates must have thought, "Samba, what is wrong with you?" It never caused any aggravation; I didn't say anything and usually laughed it off. Nobody knew I had OCD and nobody asked me about my routine. At times it was embarrassing but I just did what I did without thinking about it.

Still in Spain, after each game we'd just chuck our kit on the floor for the kit man to pick it up – well that spelled disaster for me. The kit was usually turned inside out, so I would go round the dressing room while the guys were in the shower and turn the shirts, shorts and socks the right way and put the kit in neat piles, so when the kit man came round, he wouldn't have to sort out the dirty kit. My teammates always wondered what I was doing and would stand there looking at me tidying up after them.

Although Fes took the piss at first and tried to wind me up a lot about my compulsions, he now knows not to upset me and he avoids it on the whole, although if he wants to annoy me he still touches my clothes from time to time. All my family know about my OCD; all the people close to me know how I am. At first, they thought it was funny, but it's not funny for me – it plays a big part in my life and rules it in many ways. To this day, I still see a counsellor and take tablets, but I can't control it – none of those things seems to help very much. The only thing that helps is when the house is clean and things are in order – that makes me feel settled and happy.

Recently, I've found that if I'm engaged with something, I tend to ignore my compulsions and obsessions. I need to be busy and concentrate on something and I try to ignore mess around the house (or other people's houses). Working on this book has helped because being so engaged in it means I tend to forget about other things. When I'm bored, that's when my OCD kicks in. Maybe that's the way to go in future?

Angerine has had a tough ride and for that I'm truly sorry. I don't feel great about it – it's a sad thing and it's embarrassing at times and I just wish somebody could help me. I don't mean to do it or upset anybody. Sometimes I hate myself for it – I feel like an addict and I hate it.

I'm just hoping that people who read this book don't think I'm mad or a weirdo. I'm really sorry if I've ever offended anybody along the way due to my OCD. I hope people can relate to my problems and believe it's nothing personal – I can't help it, it's just the way I am.

Chapter 14

Dreaming of the Future

"I will never, ever let you down and I will always run the race with you."

Ian Seddon
Sports Management Agent

I have the philosophy that you should never look back in anger and you should always look to the future to improve upon what you didn't do so well in your life. I can honestly say that without Angerine at the helm I would not be here writing this book and looking forward to a bright future.

Ever since I met her at the age of 18 I knew she was 'The One' and she's been my rock throughout all the good and bad times ever since. Every time I talk about her I get emotional but words can't describe how I feel about her as a person and I know I'm very blessed to have her in my life. She's my world, she really is and I couldn't wish for a better woman to call my wife because she's beautiful, both on the outside and on the inside.

I guess in a way she knew her role in our relationship from day one; I consider myself a hard person to live with in some ways and even harder to please. I'm a very tidy person and I'd go as far to say I'm OCD in that department and Angerine had to learn to live with my unusual habits, while being a footballer made it hard for her to understand my life. It's often said that, "behind every successful man there's a strong woman," and

Angerine definitely is that woman in my life. She's always had my back, even when the chips were down and has always picked up the pieces I've left behind. She's definitely had a calming effect on me and has kept me thinking positively about my own career and life in general. I know that whatever I go through in life, Angerine will be there to say, "Everything will be fine." That's just the type of person I need in my life.

It's fair to say we are very different people – Angerine is the 'realist' and I'm the 'dreamer' in our relationship, but it works. Sometimes I suggest some crazy things and she's always there to put me back in my place – maybe I need someone like that to keep me in check? I'm glad I've listened to her – if I'm honest, she's always been right (just don't tell her that). Words can't describe the impact she's had on my life. She's the one who's been there to put me back together when things didn't go to plan and she's always welcomed me with open arms, no matter how frustrated or disappointed I've been. I don't know how she does it, but she always makes me feel relaxed when I've had a bad time – I'm so lucky and I don't know what I've done to deserve it. There have been times when I've been so low, maybe after a game, but I walk through the door and the dinner's on the table, I see her big smile and it seems to make everything right again – she really takes my pain away with every little thing she does. Angerine always has a knack of saying the right things at the right time in order to make me forget my woes and makes me realise what's really important in life.

If there's been an unsung hero in my life, it's definitely Angerine. She still is today I hope she always will be because she's a special woman, the foundation of our family unit and I'm truly thankful for that.

****

There's a quote that goes along the lines of, "Sometimes people come into your life for a moment, a day or for a lifetime. It matters not the time they spent with you but how they impacted your life in that time." That is certainly true when I'm talking about my current agent, Ian Seddon.

Where do I start when I talk about Ian? Firstly, he's someone who's transformed my life since I first contacted him. Within minutes of me getting in touch, Ian responded and gave me his mobile number. We spoke that day and the first thing he asked was, "Tell me your story." A short time later we met up in London and we spoke for hours about my past and my future ambitions. I was still playing at the time, but my confidence was fairly low and I was starting to think about my retirement, so meeting Ian came just at the right moment. Some things are just meant to be, as they say.

I knew after our first meeting that Ian was a genuine guy who could be good for me and we had a good connection from day one. He'd obviously done his homework on me.

I'd only been in his camp for a matter of weeks, but he was already treating me like one of his own and he has since done so many acts of indescribable kindness. There are too many to mention here. He clearly believed in me and promised he'd 'rebrand' my image and get my story out there, which is exactly what he's done. Not only has he improved my image by securing me numerous media interviews and contracts, but he has also guided me through the difficult transition from finishing my playing career to moving into coaching.

From early on in our relationship, Ian went out of his way to support me and he introduced me to some good footballing men, including John McMahon, the former Tranmere Rovers and Shrewsbury Town manager, and Brian Little, who played for and managed Aston Villa, amongst others. Both gave up their time to help me gain new insights into the coaching side of the game, for which I'm extremely grateful.

Ian is a private man, but what he has done for me from a very early stage has been truly amazing. I soon began to realise that I was a lucky guy to have an agent who was taking care of me in such a kind and thoughtful way. I was pretty sure not many agents would have done those things for their clients, especially new ones. He's changed my philosophy and how I look at life and I can't thank him enough.

It was all down to Ian's hard work that I appeared in 'The Dream Team' and became the face of the Football Manager 2017 media campaign. He was also instrumental in helping me pursue my coaching badges. No word of a lie, Ian Seddon instigated all of the above and there's a lot more to come, believe me.

While meeting Ian touched my life in such an amazing way, meeting another person at the same time was also a special moment for me. Toby Everett was the owner of the flat in Liverpool that Ian had arranged for me to stay in for a while as we got to know each other and planned my future career. It was also a good base from which to train with the likes of John McMahon.

As it happened, Toby had gone to Glastonbury for the weekend when I first arrived at his flat, but he was due back that day, so while I was alone in his apartment I began to wonder who this guy was as he had loads of pictures of himself all over the flat. Toby arrived back that evening, covered head to toe in mud. Because I am a clean freak – on the verge of OCD – to pass the time I'd cleaned up the flat while he was away and probably moved everything around. So, I'd been there only a matter of hours and I'd re-arranged someone else's entire flat. Now that must be OCD? Obviously Toby was expecting me, so when he returned home we introduced ourselves and he went to take a shower. He must have thought his flat had been raided or something because he couldn't find anything. He also must have thought I was a complete freak. As we'd only just met, Toby was too shy and polite to say anything to me but fortunately, I'm not shy, so I apologised for re-arranging his flat and from that moment on we hit it off really well.

Incidentally, apart from Toby being a top bloke and one of the nicest, most down-to-earth guys you'd want to meet, he also happens to be a filmmaker and a director on the set of 'Hollyoaks'. After that unusual introduction, we subsequently became close mates and friends for life – he's just one of a handful of people who have touched my life in a positive and out-of-the-ordinary way.

So as you can see, in a short space of time I met two of the nicest people anyone would want to meet, and two people who have touched my life so much that I feel I am truly blessed. Without God none of the things I've been through in the last two or three years would have happened, that's for sure. I owe a lot to Ian and he has become not only my agent, but also a friend forever.

If it were not for Ian, I wouldn't be doing this book, that's for sure.

****

Ever since I was five or six, all I dreamed of was to become a professional footballer – there's that word again, 'dream'. To play for England's youth teams until under-21 level and representing Gambia have been a great joy for me as well and both of those nations played a part in helping make that dream come true. My football career has been a very special journey; a rocky road of ups and downs if you like, but I couldn't have done it without the love and support of my wife, family, friends and the special fans I've adopted along the way.

I had a difficult final few years as a player because I couldn't get back onto the pitch due to a persistent ankle injury, so I made the decision to retire at the age of 29 after 15 years in the professional game. However, unlike so many footballers when they retire, I knew exactly where my future was heading.

I'd worked with some great coaches in my time, Dick Bate being the best, but I had something to prove and something to give back to the game I loved. That's why I knew, without doubt, that the next chapter of my career was to attain my coaching badges.

I knew I had the potential to become a coach, and a good one at that. My main focus now as a coach will be centred around trying to turn all the hardships I encountered in my own career into positives for the next generation of young footballers who are about to pursue their own dream of becoming a professional. I've had so many brilliant adventures and so many disappointments along the way – but I also know I have learned from them all. The result is a wealth of knowledge, experience and a measured perspective to guide young players along the right path. Kids can learn from my story: what went wrong and what went right for Cherno Samba – and I really want people to know what I went through.

Everyone who knows me well will tell you I live and breathe football and becoming a coach is the only natural progression for me. It's always been my passion and that's why I started doing my coaching badges. I truly believe there are only a few coaches in the game who possess a greater understanding of what it's like to be the 'next big thing' of English football. I certainly know the pressure and the hype involved in being a young and talented footballer – and they were enormous – which is why I believe I'm in the best position to become a good coach, a logic that is shared by many people I know and love.

I started my coaching badges at West Ham's training ground in 2015 with the UEFA 'B' Licence, not long after announcing my retirement, and Ian Seddon was instrumental in helping me take that step. It's nice being on the other side and I can now see the hassle I gave my coaches as a youngster. I have learnt that to become a good coach you need to be confident in yourself, be understanding and have patience – all the things I didn't have as a player. It wasn't an easy passage but that's the same with anything in life I suppose – life isn't easy.

I mentioned earlier in the book that I had a brilliant strike partnership with a lad from school called James Cheeseman, before he went to Charlton at the age of 12 or 13 and I went to Millwall. Make no mistake, James influenced my life a lot during my younger days and I would like to think I did the same with his life. Apart from playing against each other a few times as youth players we hadn't really seen each other for 18 years. Fast forward to 2015 and on the first day of my Level 2 coaching course, I spotted him at the back of the classroom as I walked in. When I saw James, I admit I nearly cried – it was really a touching moment for both of us. We couldn't believe we were doing the same course at the same time and we chatted for ages about our past and where our lives had taken us.

James and I worked together throughout the course. It was like being young kids at school as we hit it off again both on and off the football pitch. As part of the course, you have to play games against each other and, guess what, James and I formed a strike partnership once more and it was as though we had never been apart. Throughout that test game, everything seemed to drop into place, just as it had 18 years previously when we played for our school or for Mottingham. We both knew each other's runs and what we were both doing. It was amazing. The other guys playing with us and against us couldn't believe the chemistry we had on the pitch. In the end we had to explain our history to the rest of the group.

It's insane to think how James touched my life again. We both spoke about how sad it was that our journeys took different paths when I went to Millwall and he went to Charlton. We both wished in a way that we'd stayed with the same team because once we separated things didn't seem the same. James's career went in a different direction to mine as he was released by Charlton at 16 and went to university to do a degree in sports science and coaching. He's now a lead strength and conditioning coach for Pentathlon GB as well as being a coach for Bristol City women's team.

If fate played a part in me linking up with James again, it also helped me to meet up with another old pal, Edrissa Sonko, who was a forward in the Gambian national side. I was sitting down in the classroom on day one of my Level 2 course and I recognised him as soon as he came into the room. We couldn't believe what was happening and embraced each other – it had been ten years since we were last together. Of all the courses he could have been on, he was on mine, and we've become very close since then.

While I'm on the subject of close friends, I'd like to mention James Ramowski, someone who recently touched my life in a very special way. One day in 2016, he called me and told me about a charity football match in Nottingham and asked me to play in it. Without hesitation I agreed to play, mainly to show my appreciation to him for helping me sort out my auntie and uncle's visas. It turned out to be a great event where the local Gambian community played the local Nottingham community. As I recall there were five games in all and the team I played for won the final.

Since that game, we have stayed in touch and got to know each other and have spoken about doing some projects together, both in Gambia and the UK.

James is a very respectable guy; generous, kind-hearted and very down-to-earth. He has done a lot of work for the Gambian community in the Nottingham area and is well respected there.

****

I've always said that once I've completed all my coaching badges – that's the UEFA A and UEFA B – and gained some valuable experience as a coach in England, I have one goal in my life and that is to become the head coach of the Gambian national side one day. Once I have secured that position my ambition will be to help them qualify for the African Cup of Nations, which has never been done before.

I know the problems the Gambian team are having, but you don't get much time to develop teams in African football, as it's more about the results. I'd need a five-year plan to achieve it because the infrastructure isn't yet in place and that needs to be looked at. You never know, the people at the top may share the same vision that I have one day. In fact, since I've linked up with Edrissa Sonko, we talk about it all the time, as it's a passion of his too. We both care about our native country and the state of football there and both of us want to do our bit to improve it – it's our inspiration. As a Gambian and having played for the country, coaching the team to try to qualify for a major tournament would be my dream and ultimate achievement.

I'd always intended to 'give something back' to Gambia in footballing terms and something happened many years ago which set me off on another dream that I'm still pursuing to this day.

It started in the year 2000 with a phone call from Harry Gerber, who was my agent back then. I was at the height of my youth career and the next 'wonderkid'; a move to Liverpool was being talked about and a prosperous career lay in front of me. I had no idea what my dreams were at the time but Harry's idea spring-boarded my imagination when he told me I needed to "Give something back to Gambia in the future." His idea was to establish a soccer academy in my home country and he was planning to go there himself to set it up in my name. I thought it was a really brilliant idea and began to get excited about the plans.

Harry kept his word and travelled to Gambia for the first time ever in 2001 and visited all of the provinces in the country looking for talented young players to invite for trials in the hope of recruiting them to play for the academy, which at that time didn't exist. As soon as he'd found enough talented youngsters, Harry registered the 'Cherno Samba Football Academy' and we were in business. Harry was there for two months and set up everything himself.

Within a year of forming the academy, things were going unbelievably well. Harry had groomed enough players to set up a new team, which we called Samger FC, a combination of our two surnames. It was good enough to qualify for the National League and within a few years the team went right to the top of that league.

The club was formed in 2003 and we based it near Serrekunda. To this day, we play in the top division of Gambian football, the Gambian Championnat National D1, and have qualified for the African Cup – the equivalent of the European Champions League – which is a massive achievement for a club that has come from nowhere and it's something that has never been done before in Gambia.

The club is structured in such a way that we look after the players' every need – we do everything from providing boots, travelling to training, a 24-seater bus, training facilities, kit and good equipment to providing decent pitches and feeding the lads with a proper, nutritious diet. It's run like any other pro-fessional club in Europe but it's more expensive as we have to provide absolutely everything for the players.

Although I'm not in Gambia for most of the year, we have a team of people who manage the club for us and we trust them. Harry's in the country most of the time during the season, though, overseeing the whole operation. We fund the club our-selves and it's not cheap. The players have their own names on their training kit and their playing shirts and they even get a monthly allowance, together with their travelling costs as most families do not earn enough to feed themselves. In fact, we also pay everyone who works for the club, including all of the non-playing staff, which totals around 40 people. We have funded all of that out of our own pockets. It has become a very expensive project over the years, but like Harry said to me when we started, it's not about the money, it's about giving some-thing back to the Gambian youths and giving them an opportu-nity and the platform to develop their talent.

The wider aim of forming the academy and the football club is to groom players to become good enough to be transferred to European clubs, or even the MLS. That part of the operation will keep the club afloat. We recently sold a player to La Liga side Granada and we've transferred players to the Hungarian and German leagues. We have a few more players who we are hoping will follow them very soon. Living and working in Europe has enabled Harry and I to build up a lot of contacts within football all over the world and we believe we are now getting pretty close to extending the operation. We have opportunities for any of the players that show promise with the club to assist their development away from the club. If any player is good enough, we will put them in the 'shop window'; it's the only way the club can operate and our aim is to make the club bigger and better by developing players who will in turn help the Gambian national team. So far, it's been working really well.

In addition, we have an on-going project in the pipeline that I believe can take Samger FC and the Cherno Samba Academy towards our next objective. We'd like to be in a position to buy land where the training pitches and facilities will be located because the rent we are currently paying has become very expensive and this an outlay we could do without. When that happens we'd like to develop accommodation where the lads can live and complete their education, whilst also developing their football on site. However, our ultimate ambition and dream for the operation is to help Gambian youth players get into the Gambian team and for Samger FC to become one of the top clubs in African football. You never know, maybe one day there will be a world football league and Samger FC could end up playing Millwall or Liverpool. Dream on, Samba!

Over the last 15 years, a lot of people in Gambia have helped the academy and the club get where they are today. I would like to publicly thank you all from the bottom of my heart – you know who you are. However, special thanks go to George Gomez, Baboucarr Camara, the honourable Alhajie Sillah,

Peter Bonu Johnson, Ebrima Manneh, Jane Joof, Alhagi Bassiru Njie, and The Gambian Football Federation for their help and support they have given the club. I would also mention the Manjai Stadium Committee, our current training facilities and the Serrekunda East Committee, the first home of the Cherno Samba Academy of Football, for all their assistance over the years.

I sometimes pinch myself to think I have my own football academy and football club – it's a dream come true and it's a dream that is alive and doing well.

****

Football management can be a short and lonely career and only the best survive. If for some reason my dream doesn't materialise, I have things to fall back on away from football. Unlike some young players, during the course of my playing career, I didn't fritter all of my money away, instead choosing to make some smart financial investments in properties and small businesses back home in Gambia, as well as the academy and football club. I did those on the back of good advice from the right people when I was young. That's a message I will tell my young players – if you earn £10,000 a week, don't spend £10,000 a week. Do what I did and get some proper advice, invest some and forget about it because you'll never know when you may have to fall back on that investment if times get hard. For me, those investments I've made over the years have made me financially comfortable now that I'm not playing and I'm assessing my future career.

However, my main aim is to get into football management. My big break in coaching came during the summer of 2017 when I received an unexpected call from the FA with an invite to be fast-tracked onto the UEFA 'A' Licence course at the Chelsea training ground at Cobham. It came out of the blue if I'm honest and, to my amazement, I was in a select group of six that included Frank Lampard and Graeme le Saux. I went there for two weeks flat-out training, and then we had to go away and do our own coaching with a club of our choice.

Just after Christmas 2017, the six of us had to go to Tottenham's training ground in Enfield, North London for a day to see how they organise their youth training set-up. We were shown around the academy by Spurs' head of coaching and development, John McDermott, a person I knew from my playing days. John explained the philosophy at the club, which includes implementing the same style of play from the youth teams all the way through to the first team. What struck me was the togetherness of the players and staff – they seem to be a very close-knit group, a bit like a family. It seemed that everyone had bought into the philosophy, which I thought was great. After the formalities, we observed and took notes on how the coaches and youth players prepare and then we went out onto the training field and saw some sessions being taken. At the end of the training we came back in and had a super lunch with the rest of the lads.

Our final briefing of the day was a Q&A with John, where we could ask questions about the day or anything else. During that briefing, the Spurs' head coach, Mauricio Pochettino and his backroom staff walked in and joined us for a while and later on we had a drink and a chat with him privately. When the rest of the lads had left, John stopped me and we chatted about our playing days and what my ambitions were for the future. Unexpectedly, John put an offer to me to join him and his coaches on a temporary basis to help out with coaching the youth team strikers at Spurs. Obviously, I jumped at the chance. With the 'A' licence you need to build up a certain number of hours' coaching before you can pass, so that was a great opportunity.

At the time of writing (January 2018) I have begun working at Spurs every Monday. It couldn't have worked out any better; indeed, I'd go as far as to say I'd have paid money to receive that opportunity, but of course working for a Premier League club is something money can't buy. I am truly grateful to John for giving me the chance because he didn't have to do that for me and he is the first person to hand me such an opportunity in coaching. In life, you never know what's around the corner, but when you're presented with a chance of a lifetime, you have to take it with both hands, or those chances may never crop up again. Working at Spurs helps me showcase my talent and I've learned so much from the other coaches that can help mould me into the type of coach I want to become. Not many people are lucky enough to be handed opportunities like this and for me there isn't a better place to be, so I'm going to embrace it all the way.

Achieving the 'A' Licence will allow me to take up any coaching role in Europe or a manager's role in the Championship and below. It will be the start of a long road to becoming a football coach. Once I'm ready to be assessed by my tutor, Jim Hicks and I've actually passed, all I will need to do is to carry on being positive, learn from my mistakes and be the best coach I can be because I'm not the finished article. I'm just very excited to start learning from other people and at the same time help youngsters learn from me.

Dreams can come true and I'm well on my way to achieving mine. Bring it on I say. I don't know what the future holds for me but I'm very much looking forward to the challenges that lie ahead.

Epilogue

*"The one thing about Cherno is that he has
always absolutely loved football"*

Jim Hicks
Head of Coaching at the PFA

Now that I've retired from playing, I really want to do my
bit to try and reverse some of the issues we have in the
game, many of which I've touched upon previously. That's
one of the main reasons for writing this book. I wanted to
tell people what a cushy life an English footballer has from
an early age and to let all those up-and-coming 'wonderkids'
know what the pitfalls can be, as I've experienced most of
them during my football journey. I wanted to let people know,
using my own experiences as a benchmark, what I think is
right and wrong with English football and how it can learn
from other countries. I think it is an English issue because
the Premier League is where everyone dreams to be – and
also where dreams are shattered. When you're so young,
you don't think about the consequences of your actions and
yes, all the money may sound cool, but the reality is that it
damages players. It damaged me personally in several ways.

Gone are the days when the academy players would clean the
first team players' boots, especially in the Premier League,
where the juniors are already earning vast sums of money.
Why would they want to clean boots when they're on £10,000
per week? You only have to look at the Spanish model to see
that their young players are groomed the right way and my

experience of La Liga confirms that belief. Young players in Spain still clean the boots of their elders in the first-team.

When I was at Millwall as a youngster, I had to clean the boots of Stephen Reid, Neil Harris and Paul Ifill after every training session and after every match. Each Christmas, I'd get excited because some of the senior players would give us a bonus (or not). You didn't do it for money but nonetheless it was good discipline. When I turned professional at Millwall, the younger players under me cleaned my boots and I'd look after them at Christmas too. It didn't do me any harm but I think it's all but disappeared in top-flight clubs, which is a shame. The Premier League can learn a lot from La Liga about how to prepare young footballers for adulthood and promotion to the first team.

Having experienced the highs and lows of professional football for 15 years, I really believe I'm in a good place to advise the next Wayne Rooney, Dele Alli or the next Cherno Samba on how to become a proper person and still fulfil your dreams, centred around good old fashioned values like hard work and determination. It's not all about trying to get to the top in one year, two years or even five years; it takes time and experience to get there. Yes, it's appealing for a 15-year-old to look at the likes of Dele Alli and the new breed of 'wonderkid' and want to replicate their rise to fame, but I can testify that there are lots of people out there who will want a piece of you and will entice you to fall into the same traps that so many other footballing prospects have fallen into over the years. There are hundreds of players who have seen the bright lights and glamour that surround the modern game, me included, but have fallen foul of them and out of the game almost as quickly as they came into it.

The flash cars, big houses, attractive women and the expensive designer clothes are the carrots dangling in front of these young players and it's so tempting, but it comes with a price. "Too much, too young," is a term that has been used in the media to describe English football's 'culture of reward without opportunity'. It is taking the hunger out of young players and creating teenage millionaires with bleak futures. Young footballers are now seen as 'commodities' in the modern game and, to me, it's a crying shame. I have a concern that young lads have little hope of actually living the dreams they are being sold by some agents from a very early age. This is obviously a generalisation and there are exceptions to the rule, but it is an increasing problem in the game we all love.

The overriding issue here is money. Young lads are secured at clubs on silly amounts from the age of 12 or 13, or even younger – I know because I've stood in their boots. Not only is it harming the development of young footballers, but it's actually ruining lives too. I was barely a teenager when I started to realise how famous I was going to be. When I was a kid at Millwall, I didn't know any better and I just wanted to play football, but the pressure was on me from an early age and I was expected to deliver a consistently high level of performance over a number of years, which is nigh on impossible. Young players these days are thrown into the cauldron from day one and expected to perform week in, week out. Add into the melting pot the explosion in social media and it means players are now directly accessible to everyone – what's stopping people saying whatever they want when they're hiding behind their mobile device? For that player, they are defenceless because they are representing their club and can't complain because they are earning thousands of pounds a week. If a top player complains they just get the response, "How can you be stressed on £30,000-a-week?" as if the salary makes the slightest scrap of difference to their state of mind. The general population would find it incredibly difficult to cope with that scenario.

Apathy is a word often used in football. For young players earning silly amounts of money from an early age, it can reduce their focus on becoming better players and create a sense that the game already owes them a living – even at the age of 12! It's not unusual to see teenagers earning up to £30,000 a week and that figure will probably rise until something is done to stop the crazy sums thrown at these lads. A grown man who earns that sort of money would probably go off the rails in some way, let alone a 12-year-old kid who is still forming his own personality and learning what life is all about.

Young lads who are brought into a club at seven years old, training four nights a week, playing in matches that they're told are important, are then released at 18. Then there's the over-zealous parent who's encouraging him as well and maybe giving him the wrong advice. For young players, there's no escape from the pressure football now creates. Is it any wonder some of them run out of steam at a young age? If I had my life again, I wouldn't want to be so famous so early in my career – I would have been happy being one of those kids you didn't hear about, and who emerges from the pack later on, without all the fuss and hype. I'd like to think I would have done a whole lot of things differently, and better. On reflection, being so far above everyone else in my age group actually didn't help me. I was scoring goals, left, right and centre and instead of working harder, I felt I didn't need to and told myself I'd already made it at the age of 16 or 17. That was the wrong attitude completely.

There are the exceptions such as a Marcus Rashford or Tom Davies who have come through the ranks and made it into the so-called 'big-time'. However, the odds of a young footballer actually progressing to play in the Premier League are extremely low, with a success rate of less than one in several thousand becoming a Premier League player, let alone a superstar. Even those who do make it to professional level, joining an academy at the age of 16, have the odds stacked against them to break into the first-team.

With money being the major motivator, it's a fact that far too many childhoods are being lost to football and that there are far too few careers to show for the sacrifice. If you're a young, aspiring footballer reading this book or you have been through this journey just like me, ask yourself a question – is the sacrifice worth making?

It's a tough world out there but I'm fortunate to have come out the other end and my experiences have made me a better, more rounded person. I now have a purpose in life and aspirations to become a qualified coach and I intend to teach young players how to become not only a better player but also to become a better human being. Not too many football coaches have lived the life I have and come out the other end still with their pride and dignity in tact. I really believe that there couldn't be anyone any better qualified than me to be a football coach, and a life coach to boot. If I can give something back to those young talented footballers – some of the things I didn't have, in terms of advice and protection, from someone who cares about them – then that will be a positive. If I can prevent even just one of those lads from making the same mistakes that I did, then it will have been worthwhile.

Football is a glamorous, multi-billion pound industry and the potential rewards are unbelievable, but it's a short career, so those who pursue that career need to have good people around them who can help them make their way in life and aren't just in it for themselves or to line their own pockets. That's my motivation for writing this book.

I'd like to think that people will read this and think to themselves, "Wow, I've heard about this Cherno Samba guy and what he says is right you know – football is full of people wanting to exploit you and make money from your talents. I'm not going to make the same mistakes that Cherno did."

I'm really looking forward to the new challenges that lie ahead of me. I have a renewed energy, a positive outlook and a brand new life. I'm enjoying every minute of every day and that's something I couldn't always say when I was at the height of my career.

I hope you've enjoyed reading my story and if you're a young player starting out on a new career, I wish you all the best and I hope you are able to learn something from my experiences.

Good luck and God bless.

Cherno Samba

Testimonials

The author would like to thank everyone who has contributed to this section, with their fabulous stories of Cherno and their times spent with him throughout the years.

Dick Bate
Former England Youth Team Head Coach

My brief as an England coach was to identify players who would be good enough to play for the national side at youth level. Young players were identified from across the country and invited for trials at Lilleshall. The trials consisted of 11-a-side games against different opponents. When I watched Cherno, I soon took note of his energy and his industrious work-rate, but more importantly he would always bring others into play, which was a good strength at that age so I identified him as a team player – Cherno always liked to push forward with or without the ball and would link up with others.

I would say his first touch was adequate – not bad, but not his strongest point. However, he'd often receive the ball at speed so it could be said his movement may have had an effect on his touch at times. His main strength lay in the penalty area, where he would cause defenders all sorts of problems by shifting the ball and his body very quickly over short distances. Those are a few qualities I liked about Cherno back then.

Cherno was a natural born footballer and possessed an undying love for the game and a desire to improve every time he put on a pair of boots. He always tried to make himself a better player every time he trained and every time he played and that is a magnificent quality to have.

In terms of his future career, Cherno **WILL** have a life in football, that's for sure. Although it's difficult to envisage anyone as a potential future coach when they're 14 or 15-year-old, it doesn't surprise me at all that Cherno wants to become a coach.

Everybody who knows Cherno knows that he loves the game. He has worked hard to achieve what he did in football and at the same time tried hard to make sense of the game, which at times can be cruel. I know Cherno is undertaking his 'A' Licence (at the time of writing) but I've never seen him work as a coach, so it's hard for me to comment on exactly what will make him stand out from the others. However, I'd imagine his ability to get on with people and his need to be respected would stand him in good stead to establish himself as a coach in the game. People will listen to him and he will be good with everyone he comes into contact with, on and off the field, because of that positive presence he has around people. It could be said that Cherno smiles easily and has a certain 'charm', which are important mannerisms to have. I'm sure Cherno will continue to establish a good rapport with everyone he meets because he's such a happy lad who has had a good foundation and understanding of the game, which will also help him to progress. In reality, being a coach is all about establishing relationships with people, reassuring them that you're on their side – which he would certainly do – and letting people know you know about the game – which I'm sure he does anyway.

I can see him being a coach, and a good one at that. Once Cherno passes his badges, it will be up to him to decide where he works and what level he wants to reach – does he want to work with young development players or be a results-based coach within a club? The two are very different and they both have very different approaches to coaching but I'm sure

Cherno will know the direction he wants to take once he is in that position. He will be a good learner and in my mind would be excellent either way because he has so many of the qualities required to become a good coach in the game he loves so much.

Jim Hicks
Head of Coaching at the PFA

My abiding memories of Cherno as a schoolboy at Millwall will always be of this larger than life character and a very affable lad, who was never 'big-time' and always got on with everyone. He had a very infectious habit of being in and around football and always wanted to join in. Just before Cherno joined the ranks at Millwall as a schoolboy, I was working on the community programme and I would go into his school to run football sessions. Cherno was in a group with some other, very good players so we would have some unbelievably good games and some great sessions.

Those days stick out for me and particularly one day in mid-winter when I was running a session practising diving headers and we wet ourselves with laughter because we were pinging balls into the box and we were diving full length into the muddy penalty area, trying to head the ball into the net. Cherno was one of those lads who absolutely loved it and it didn't worry him getting soaking wet and muddy.

The one thing about Cherno is that he has always absolutely loved football and at that time he wasn't interested in it for financial or career reasons – he just wanted to play and to learn. That's what I remember him for mostly when he played football as a schoolboy.

The other thing that sticks in my mind is that he was much, much bigger than most of the other lads in his school year, and probably most of the years above his age group, too. We had a picture of Cherno on the wall at Millwall taken during a school football tournament, where he had his elbow resting on top of another kid's head – the other lad was of the same age. Cherno was probably biologically 17 at the time, even though he would have been 12 or 13, and the other kid was maybe biologically 12, which was his own age. Cherno was so much more developed than his peers.

After Cherno signed for Millwall on a full-time contract I had no real connection with him and he later left the club to pursue his career elsewhere. The next time I had any sort of contact with him was 15 years later when he started his UEFA B coaching course at West Ham's training ground in 2015. When I saw his name on the list, I wasn't really surprised because he'd previously made some contact with the PFA a few months earlier, but it was great to see him nonetheless. His name sent a positive ripple through our department because Neil Bailey, who worked at the PFA in the North-West of England, knew of Cherno from his days working at Manchester United, where Cherno had taken a trial when he was 15. The news created a bit of a buzz about Cherno Samba in our department, so that was quite nice.

Like many youngsters, Cherno was touted to be 'the next big thing' but never really fulfilled that enormous potential – but to be fair, hardly anyone ever does. Not everyone can be a top player – it's just not possible. Cherno's story is very relevant now because every single kid who goes to a club thinks they have the opportunity to become the next Ian Wright or the next Alan Shearer or whomever you want to name. Sure, they have the 'potential' to do that, but not everyone actually fulfils it. I think it's really relevant that someone like Cherno, who has been through the process, can actually tell his story so that youngsters can hopefully learn from some of the things he did or didn't do during his football career.

There aren't enough stories out there about people who under-achieve or the reasons why that happens. We all see kids with talent but we don't always see the account of why they didn't get to the level they should have. That's why I really believe he will go on and make a very good coach, once he has learnt he can't be the jester all the time. He will make it as a coach because has a real passion for the game, he wants to learn and wants to be good at it. He's got a great rapport with people, which is a big plus in his favour and he is a very personable character indeed. Cherno is an infectious guy and if he can learn how to manage that sort of 'buzz' – that electricity he has when he's around people – and uses it to his advantage in a positive way, in my mind that can be a very powerful skill for him to have. Certainly, if he can become a good, young, black coach, he can do very well indeed because they aren't ten-a-penny.

Kenny Swain
Former England Under-16 Coach

My connection with Cherno at England was probably for about one year, when he was with the Under-16s before I left the FA in 2004. From what I remember, he was an interesting character – a solid and reliable lad with a bubbly personality who was good around the dressing room. Cherno was hard working and always loved training. More importantly, he was good for the team because he was a goal scorer.

Cherno was a lean and fit lad, with potential to grow into a formidable striker. He definitely had pace – an important attribute for any modern-day striker and that was effectively his game, to run at defenders and score. There were other strikers around at that time, the likes of Darren Bent and David Bentley spring to mind, but Cherno was different to them.

At that time, it looked like he had prospects for his future but for whatever reason, he didn't reach that potential in England and that was a great shame in my eyes because he could have been excellent.

Harry Gerber
Cherno's former coach and agent

I first noticed Cherno when he was 10 years old, whilst I was watching my Assistant Manager's son play football for a local side in the Peckham area of South-East London. Everyone in the area was talking about this Cherno Samba lad and his footballing ability.

I remember the first time I saw Cherno play – I was very impressed with his football ability and I wanted him to play for my team, Mottingham Youth FC, as I wanted all the best players in the area and I really thought I could help him develop his game.

My club was a disciplined set-up and full of boys of Cherno's age; however, what really impressed me about him was that he was a fast learner and he was able to pick up things quicker than the other players. After only a few weeks, he began to realise what being a footballer was all about and that it wasn't all about kicking a ball around the streets with your mates. Even at that age, Cherno only had one thing on his mind – and that was to score goals. There were times I had to restrict his game in training, and in matches, because it was too easy for him and I had to get him to involve the other players in the team. Cherno was further advanced than most of the other players of his age group in the area and a lot of people said they could see he had the ability to become a top-class professional football player, even at that age.

A few months after I started coaching Cherno at Mottingham Youth FC, his school got to the inter-schools final at Wembley and it was there he started to make his name. Even though they lost that game, he was one of the players that really stood out. Playing for Mottingham at the age of 11, Cherno was up against many good young players, including the likes of Kieran Richardson and Glen Johnson to name two, in a league that was very competitive – and we soon became one of the teams to beat in the area. Our club was getting a lot of recognition locally, and we sometimes played games against professional clubs like Millwall, Wimbledon and West Ham Under-12s. In hindsight, that proved productive because most of the players ended up training with professional clubs.

Although many of the clubs we played against were interested in Cherno, it was Millwall who invited myself and the team to look at their set-up – and that led to me leaving Mottingham to join Millwall as a coach, along with Cherno and some of the other lads. I continued coaching Cherno at Millwall until he joined the Under-16s and I left shortly afterwards, but I then became his adviser and his 'official' agent.

After Cherno was chosen to represent England, his profile increased to a level that was attracting interest from Premier League clubs. The national media were also becoming aware of Cherno as he starting scoring goals for England Schoolboys, which were repeatedly shown on TV. This promoted his profile further and clubs started contacting Millwall on a regular basis, with firm interest from Liverpool in particular.

A short time after, Millwall gave permission for Cherno to visit Liverpool, Leeds United and Manchester United to decide which club he preferred. However, during his visit to Liverpool, while watching the reserves play, the media saw Cherno wearing a Liverpool jacket and the next day the media broke a story that he was about to sign for Liverpool. The visit and the situation got blown out of all proportion, because even though I wasn't party to the negotiations, I knew nothing had been agreed at that time. The story appeared in local and national papers and this did not help Cherno as it only increased his value, and I think it must have unsettled Millwall somewhat, because they then knew they had a special player on their hands – and I think they then reconsidered their position as they did not want to lose him.

I know Liverpool were very interested in signing him and Cherno wanted to sign for them, despite the fact he was a

Manchester United fan. I believe Liverpool was his preferred club, but Millwall were not able to agree terms with them – or any of the clubs interested in him at the time.

After the media frenzy, things got a bit out of hand over the following six months, with Cherno and I trying everything to push through his transfer. An FA tribunal got involved and it broke Cherno's heart when he was deprived of his dream move. I truly believe that Cherno never recovered from that. Even though he didn't play for Millwall for those six months, he continued to represent England and was allowed to train at Arsenal's training ground to keep fit.

Throughout my time as Cherno's mentor, friend and agent I have always tried to do the very best for him, but I was extremely surprised and disappointed that Millwall released him at the age of 19 and that hurt me considerably because of the huge opportunity that he was deprived of a few years earlier. During this period, both his parents and I became obsessed with finding a new club that would help Cherno with his football development. I was able to secure a contract with the Spanish club, Cádiz to try and get his career back on track. Cádiz treated Cherno very well and looked after him like a son – they knew his past situation and they knew he had the technical ability to be a good player in Spain. As soon as he had settled in, he quickly became a popular character and his confidence returned, even though he seemed lonely at times whenever I visited him in Spain.

Growing up in an urban inner-city environment, and with some people who may have led him astray, it's testament to him that he's never been in trouble with the police when trouble was all around him at a young age. Cherno turned to football, kept his dignity in tact and for me, that says it all. I once told Cherno that he deserved to earn a living out of football, whether it was playing or coaching, because he had a natural football talent and it would have been a waste if he had turned his back on it, only to follow some of his mates into a different life. Even after all he has been through, he has remained resolute.

To conclude, I have known Cherno for over 23 years and during that time, I have seen him develop from a little boy at primary school who had the world at his feet, to a teenager who had his dreams shattered and now to a family man, who most parents would be proud of. I've seen what Cherno has been through at first hand – the ups and downs in his career and the impact that all these things have had on him – and his family.

I don't think there are too many people around who would have come through what Cherno has endured during his short period in football. I am so pleased that he had a strong network of support from his family and friends around him. The grounding from his mother and father has proved invaluable to him and has helped him to overcome all the disappointments he's had in his life. I also believe that having positive friends around him during his teenage years has brought a positive aspect and direction to his life when he most needed it. However, I also believe that the person that has had the biggest influence in Cherno's life over the years is his wife, who I know has been his strength and it's a blessing that he's turned out the way he has and become the person that he is today – a decent person with great values in life and I love and respect him for that.

I know he is now currently doing his coaching badges and has aspirations to become a top football coach. I am really proud of him and, regardless of all his trials and tribulations, he still has the drive to want to pursue a career in football to help other youngsters. I am extremely confident that he will succeed in his new career as a football coach as I believe he has so much to offer.

Mel Stein
Sports Lawyer and Author

As a 15-year-old, Cherno was an extra-ordinary footballer. Everybody at the time thought he was going to be the 'next big thing'. He was a big lad, mobile and incredibly fit. As a person,

Cherno was a lovely boy, polite as they come, respectful and everything most modern-day footballers aren't.

I first met Cherno through his then agent, Harry Gerber, who introduced me to him because he had some issues at his club, Millwall. As I recollect, Millwall apparently didn't know Cherno was going to Liverpool to seek a move and later found out when he was filmed wearing a Liverpool jacket and Millwall didn't like that – then all hell broke loose. Following that incident, Millwall didn't treat Cherno too well and priced him out of his dream move. As I recall, a fee couldn't be agreed and it went to tribunal, but Millwall refused to sell their star player.

Subsequently, I involved one of my litigation partners at Clinton's to act on Cherno's behalf. I don't remember the details of the case or how it got resolved, but I do think Millwall backed off but subsequently didn't do anything to develop Cherno as a player, so his career was on hold throughout the remainder of his Millwall contract – or maybe it went into reverse. By standing up to the club, Cherno's reputation took a dive. As a very young man, Cherno didn't cope with it very well and it all ended up as an unfortunate turn of events.

Later on in his career, Cherno had problems at the start of his Málaga career as the club hadn't paid him and I helped him out of that situation, as I recall.

In my view, Cherno was an opportunity lost to football – I genuinely believe he could have played for a Premier League club and for England. He could have been every bit as good as some of the strikers England have had in recent times and I think it's a tragedy for football that his career wasn't allowed to take off when it wasn't his fault.

"All praises are due to Allah our Lord for giving me the strength and wisdom to be able to tell my story. May it be beneficial to the whole of humanity, especially the youth.

Thank you all for the support.

God Bless.

Cherno Samba.

During the production of this book, the
world lost a truly great man.

Dick Bate sadly passed away on 25th April 2018.

I will miss my 'Football Father' so much.

RIP Dick Bate.